Mark Witham
1996

GO
THE
DISTANCE

THE MAKING OF A PROMISE KEEPER

JOHN TRENT
with

CHARLES COLSON · JACK HAYFORD · BILL MᶜCARTNEY · JESSE MIRANDA
GARY OLIVER · LUIS PALAU · JOHN PERKINS · RANDY PHILLIPS
PETE RICHARDSON · GARY SMALLEY · STU WEBER

PUBLISHING
Colorado Springs, Colorado

GO THE DISTANCE
Copyright © 1996 by Promise Keepers. All rights reserved. International copyright secured.

Library of Congress Cataloging-in-Publication Data
Trent, John T.
    Go the distance / John Trent.
        p. cm.
    ISBN 1-56179-435-X
    1. Promise Keepers (Organization).   2. Men—Religious life.   3. Husbands—Religious life.
4. Fathers—Religious life.   5. Family—Religious life.   6. Christian life.   I. Title.
BV970.P76T74   1996
248.8'42—dc20

                          96-11855
                            CIP

Published by Focus on the Family Publishing, Colorado Springs, CO 80995. Distributed in the U.S.A. and Canada by Word Books, Dallas, Texas.

Promise Keepers and the PK logo are Registered Service Marks of Promise Keepers.

Unless otherwise noted, Scripture quotations are from the HOLY BIBLE, NEW INTERNATIONAL VERSION ®: Copyright © 1973, 1978, 1984 by the International Bible Society. Used by permission of Zondervan Publishing House. All rights reserved. Quotations labeled *Living Bible* are from *The Living Bible*, © 1971. Used by permission of Tyndale House Publishers, Inc., Wheaton, IL 60189. All rights reserved. Quotations labeled NKJV are from *The New King James Version*, copyright © 1979, 1980, 1982 by Thomas Nelson, Inc., Publishers. Used by permission. All rights reserved. Quotations labeled *The Message* are from *The Message: The New Testament in Contemporary English*, by Eugene H. Peterson, © 1993 by NavPress. Used by permission. All rights reserved. Quotations labeled KJV are from the King James Version of the Bible. Quotations labeled NASB are from the *New American Standard Bible*, © 1960, 1963, 1968, 1971, 1973, 1975, and 1977 by The Lockman Foundation. Used by permission.

People's names and certain details of the case studies in this book have been changed to protect the privacy of the individuals involved. However, the facts of what happened and the underlying principles have been conveyed as accurately as possible.

No part of this publication may be reproduced, stored in a retrieval system, or transmitted in any form or by any means—electronic, mechanical, photocopy, recording, or otherwise—without prior permission of the publisher.

Promise Keepers is represented by the literary agency of Alive Communications, 1465 Kelly Johnson Blvd., Suite 230, Colorado Springs, CO 80920.

Editor: Larry K. Weeden
Front cover design: Bradley L. Lind

Printed in the United States of America

96 97 98 99/10 9 8 7 6 5 4 3 2

Contents

Foreword

by
Randy Phillips

S peaking before a packed-in crowd at a Fellowship of Christian Athletes breakfast just days before Nebraska beat Florida for the 1996 college football national championship, Cornhuskers receivers coach Ron Brown contrasted two types of players he sees every day. One type has turned Nebraska into a perennial contender, he said. The other rarely sees action.

"As a coach, I'm not interested in 'part-time' players," said Brown, a devoted Christian. "Over the course of a long season, part-time players will let you down—*guaranteed!* I'm looking for full-time players who will show up ready to play every day, every play. Men who are willing to do what it takes in practice also have what it takes to win in a game." Then Brown surprised the audience. *"And I'm here to tell you that God is looking for full-time players, too!"*

Go the Distance, a Book for Full-Time Players

Since 1991, God has done so many amazing things through this movement called Promise Keepers. He took an idea planted in the hearts of two men and grew it into a nationwide mobilization of Christian brothers hungry for revival both in their personal lives and throughout the Body of Christ. So far, more than a million men in stadiums coast to coast have embraced God's

Word, pledged to raise Jesus Christ as the standard in their homes and communities, and purposed to break down walls that separate them from God, their families, and one another. The Lord has truly done "exceedingly above all we could ask or think," so much so that we now find ourselves breathlessly trying to keep up with Him.

What you are about to read, Go the Distance, is a book for men who don't want merely to stand on the sidelines and talk about living their lives for Jesus Christ. It's for men who will pay the price of godliness every day so that when "game day" comes, they're ready and equipped to give it their all.

The mission of Promise Keepers has never been simply to host conferences for thousands. Along with its exponential growth has come a deeper understanding of how Promise Keepers is to serve and proceed into the next century. Now more than ever, we're convicted that God is calling Promise Keepers to equip men to *keep* the promises they make and grow in Christlikeness. The primary purpose of this book, therefore, is to lay out life-changing goals for every Christian man and help you get started in the process.

We're calling multitudes of men, over the next 25 years, to actively live out the seven promises of a Promise Keeper!

Whether you're a long-term Promise Keeper, you've attended only a single event, or you've just now become aware of this ministry, our prayer is that you view your participation as a lifetime commitment rather than a one-time experience or annual rite. With Go the Distance, we're asking men of every age, color, and social class to peer down the road of life and ask themselves where they want to be as they prepare to cross the finish line. Will there be regrets or fulfillment, spiritual mediocrity or dynamic, intimate relationship with Jesus Christ? Will our society have disintegrated around us, or will a unified, empowered church be exerting a healing influence?

And what role will you play? As a man who calls himself a Promise Keeper, are you prepared to be a *full-time* player, counted on to go the distance and finish well for Christ? Are you the type of player who will let go of prejudices and opinions to step across racial and denominational boundaries? Are you the type of player who will look out for another's interests rather than your own? Those are the standards to which Jesus calls us throughout the New Testament, and they're the goals Promise Keepers is calling men to pursue over the next 25 years. (If you're not sure where you stand with God, please read the section "Wandering Prodigals Welcome" on pp. 53-54.)

Our Commitment to Provide You with the "Right Equipment"

By asking God to raise up multitudes of men who are totally sold out to Jesus Christ over the next quarter century, we realize we're asking God for a miracle—one that can happen only as the Holy Spirit imparts life-changing power in hearts ripe to discover and receive God's perfect will and the truth of His Word. By calling men to be full-time players for Christ—not just conference attenders—Promise Keepers hopes to complement what God is already doing at events by providing men with the right equipment to stay in the game.

One such tool is *The Seven Promises of a Promise Keeper*, a book defining the core commitments of a Promise Keeper. (Those seven promises, which also provide the foundation for this book, grew out of an intense time of prayer and discussion among our staff and board of directors a few years ago.) Next is *The Power of a Promise Kept*, a collection of testimonies from men who made and began to keep their promises, and whose lives were transformed in the process. Now, with *Go the Distance*, we believe the most important tool is in place. *Go the Distance* is designed to teach practical, daily principles of godly living and help men get from where they are to where they want to be.

Among the authors is Bill McCartney, founder of Promise Keepers, who will paint a portrait of a society in which a multitude of men are keeping their promises. He will also explain the starting point for all meaningful change—*brokenness*. Jack Hayford will recount painful seasons of testing that spawned a devotional life that revolutionized his walk with God. Other valuable insights will be given by Gary Smalley, Luis Palau, John Perkins, Chuck Colson, Stu Weber, Jesse Miranda, and Gary Oliver—all godly men who have spent decades working out the seven promises in their lives and ministries. Throughout the book, John Trent will provide a road map for applying godly principles in your own experience.

Because you've bought this book, you've identified yourself as a man committed both to *knowing* Christ and to *growing with* Him. My fervent prayer is that *Go the Distance* serves God's purposes in two ways: as a strengthening tool to set you on the lifelong path of becoming more like Jesus Christ, and as an encouragement to "go the distance" as a full-time player for Him—every step, every play, every day. I'll see you at the finish line.

Randy T. Phillips
President, Promise Keepers

God Is Calling Us
to a Higher Love

by
Bill McCartney

What would it look like 25 years from now if a multitude of men would make—and live out!—each of the seven promises of a Promise Keeper?

Not so long ago, God revealed my emotional dullness to a budding crisis in my marriage. In the nick of time, He showed me that I had been blind to the pain of my wife, Lyndi. It's a humbling admission. Imagine, the founder of a men's movement dedicated to honoring Jesus and family didn't have his own act together at home! The man who has stood on platforms before stadiums full of men, demonstrating how to pray over one's wife and children, was not in touch with the heartaches of his own family.

When I think of the times I've told men to kneel with their wives each morning and say a prayer of love and healing over them, or challenged them to carefully prepare their hearts at the end of each day so they might *give them up* totally to their wives, it makes me shudder. I've spoken at length and even written a book about the trap of chasing a career at the expense of family. I've repented as publicly as a man can do, even bringing Lyndi up on stage with me to hug, kiss, and honor her as my beloved wife. How could I have *not* recognized the signs? How did the Lord allow me to continue preaching on Christian family values?

I believe many men are in the same condition, allowing our promises and good intentions to disguise the ugly truth. I didn't realize it, but I was blowing it in my most important ministry—to the woman God gave me and told me to love as Christ loves the church.

In spite of all my convicting speeches, I was still living *my* dream, chasing *my* goals. I relished the heady combination of coaching a nationally ranked football team *and* my visionary role in the ministry of Promise Keepers. I would switch automatically from the time-consuming, high-pressure grind of college football to a challenging summer Promise Keepers schedule. For a hard driver like myself (and many of you), it doesn't get much better. When I was home, Lyndi got whatever I had left over, which wasn't much.

Then came the Sunday morning when God jolted me awake. A guest speaker, a pastor named Jack Taylor, came to our church with a message that challenged my whole way of thinking. He started his sermon with a simple question: "Do you want to know about the character of a man? Do you *really* want to know about a man's character? Then look into the face of his wife. Whatever he has invested in her or withheld from her will be reflected in her countenance."

His comments made me squirm. He then proceeded to teach from Scripture. Beginning in the book of Genesis and ending in the New Testament, he showed that God has *mandated* that every man draw his wife to splendor in Jesus Christ. I turned to look at Lyndi, and what I saw sent shivers down my spine. Her face was sad and empty. Instead of splendor I saw pain; instead of contentment I saw torment. Rather than reflecting the glory of a rich, satisfying life, she appeared totally drained and unfulfilled. In all her years of following me down my personal path of achievement, it seemed as if she had lost her own way. How could this be? What neglect!

I knew then, for the sake of our marriage and the testimony of Jesus Christ in my life, that I had to choose. I knew I must resign as head coach of the Colorado Buffaloes—an announcement that shocked the sports world. Many asked incredulously, "How could a coach at the top of his profession just walk away?" People called me crazy when they heard I was simply going to devote myself to my wife. But I wanted to do my part as a husband so that God could bring Lyndi back to her glory, and I have not regretted it. Today, the sparkle is coming back in my wife's eye. She's beginning to radiate God's splendor.

I tell that story not to grab attention or soothe my conscience but to reveal the work God has begun in me. I want to explain how God has started to "break" me of my underlying pride and selfishness. Through many gut-wrenching seasons of life, I have thankfully come to realize that until I come to an end of myself, I'll never be of any use to Jesus. He has shown me in painful, hard lessons the true path to fellowship with the Lord—it's the path of *brokenness*. It's the path of surrender, of sacrifice, of realizing we have *no* rights as Christians. It's a path Scripture tells us all men must travel as they mature in Christ. And it's a road men must walk if the church is to fulfill its mission as God's chosen vessel for healing and salvation to those who don't know Him. Men, we must be *crucified with Christ* (see Gal. 2:20).

It's Time to Take Inventory

Each morning when I awake, my first conscious thought is always the same. I immediately ask God for His direction for Promise Keepers, for His strategy to end racism, and for what He would have me say if given the opportunity to speak. As Promise Keepers enters its second five-year phase, I believe it's fitting for us as individuals, and as an organization, to take a hard look at ourselves—a thorough spiritual inventory. Where have we been? Where are we going? What is the condition of our hearts?

I've been asked, for the purposes of *Go the Distance,* to envision a society 25 years from now in which multitudes of men have made and *lived out* each of the seven promises of a Promise Keeper. When I try to imagine it, I see our planet transformed in wondrous ways. I see a new generation of godly fathers, healthy marriages, and sturdy families setting a biblical standard for a searching world. I see brothers in Christ locking arms across the gulf of race and denomination to bring hope and healing to the inner cities. And I see a revived, unified church spreading a fire of spiritual awakening across our land. It's a glorious vision, and by God's grace it will one day come to pass. But right now I can't begin to see that far. Why? Because I've been blind to the true depth of my brother's pain. I wonder how many men who consider themselves to be committed Promise Keepers are still functionally blind—or indifferent—to their brother's pain. Let me tell you a story that helped me see just how far I personally have to go.

There are few jobs as fascinating as the one I've held since coming to work full time for Promise Keepers in June 1995. My primary responsibility has been to travel to major cities and meet with small groups of minority clergymen, encouraging them to recognize that Promise Keepers is a movement of God, not man, and pleading with them not to let it pass them by. I ask them to experience a conference and see for themselves how God is moving in men's hearts.

In one such recent meeting in New York City, I began to tell a story about my relationship with my children. It was a painful disclosure about some of my shortcomings as a father. All of a sudden (and to my embarrassment), I began to weep uncontrollably—I just lost it and couldn't stop. Within seconds, several of the pastors started weeping, triggering a release of cleansing and conviction by the Holy Spirit. I had a sense that there had been significant healing between myself and some of the African-American pastors.

But before the meeting ended, as we were still talking, I saw a black preacher stand and begin walking toward me. He stopped right in front of me and stared me in the eye. Then he pointed his finger and screamed, "You don't know what pain is!"

It was a powerful jolt. I wasn't prepared for it. With building intensity, the pastor continued, "I experience pain 10 times a week that is so far beyond anything you will ever know. *Don't* come in here telling me about your pain."

We stood, looking at each other, until he turned and silently walked away. I was speechless. In no way did I feel diminished or wronged. But in that instant, I felt he was right. Though I've had my share of difficulties, compared to that man, I *didn't* know pain.

I didn't know what it was like to be devalued for the color of my skin or denied opportunities for which I was fully qualified. I didn't understand what it was to be forced to the sidelines of a white-oriented culture. My life has been blessed beyond measure. I was hired to coach at one of the nation's most successful and high-profile football programs; I had been rewarded financially, and I have a wonderful wife and family. In that incredible moment, I saw as never before that there is pain floating just beyond our periphery of such incredible proportions that most of us can't comprehend it.

Contending for the Faith in Oneness of Spirit

Where will the men of God be as the world sinks deeper into spiritual decay and moral chaos? Will they be marching the front lines in unity and courage, upholding the truth, often against violent opposition? Or will they be immobilized by pride and prejudice, blind to the pain of the perishing and indifferent to those who think or look differently? Almighty God is looking for men to lead His church into the next century who know and love His Son with unbridled passion, who have set aside criticisms and judgments to join hands across racial and denominational lines. He's looking for men who are in love with His Word, who will boldly contend for the faith in oneness of spirit. If the church is to be His chosen vessel of healing and salvation in these last days, He needs men rooted and built up in Jesus Christ.

In praying for God to refine and break the men He has called to be true promise keepers, I see three passages of Scripture as key for the Body of Christ if it's to be a catalyst for godly change. As you read the following passages, consider them not as unattainable ideals but as hard goals for the next two and a half decades.

> *Philippians 1:27:* "Whatever happens, conduct yourselves in a manner worthy of the gospel of Christ. Then, whether I come and see you or only hear about you in my absence, I will know that you stand firm in one spirit, contending as one man for the faith of the gospel."

> *Colossians 2:6-7:* "So then, just as you received Christ Jesus as Lord, continue to live in him, rooted and built up in him, strengthened in the faith as you were taught, and overflowing with thankfulness."

> *Colossians 3:11:* "Here there is no Greek or Jew, circumcised or uncircumcised, barbarian, Scythian, slave or free, but Christ is all, and is in all."

Where You Go I Will Go!

Collectively, those verses echo God's urgent call to men, telling us how we're going to be the ministry Almighty God is raising us up to be. We must be men who will lay down our lives for our brothers.

The book of Ruth poignantly illustrates this picture of self-sacrificing devotion. Ruth struck a pledge with her deceased husband's mother that became a lesson in selflessness for the ages. She said, "Don't urge me to leave you or to turn back from you. Where you go I will go, and where you stay I will stay.

Your people will be my people and your God my God. Where you die I will die, and there I will be buried. May the LORD deal with me, be it ever so severely, if anything but death separates you and me" (Ruth 1:16-17).

That is the spirit of oneness worthy of the gospel of Christ. Men who refuse to leave their brother's side no matter what, who carry one another's burdens and announce to the world, "Where you go I will go. Your people are my people. Where you die I will die"—*those* are the men God will use to transform a culture. *That's* standing firm in one spirit. God expects nothing less. The Bible instructs, "Do nothing out of selfish ambition or vain conceit, but in humility consider others better than yourselves. Each of you should look not only to your own interests, but also to the interests of others" (Phil. 2:3-4).

Only as we begin to demonstrate this spirit will we start to contend as one man for the faith of the gospel. Only as we recognize we're going to spend all eternity together—black, white, brown, red, poor, rich, Baptist, Presbyterian, Lutheran, Pentecostal—will we find the Spirit's indwelling courage to lay down our lives for one another. Only as we accept that we have no value or purpose outside our shared identity in Christ will we bear fruit that has lasting value.

The choice is ours. We can continue going our own way, turning our brothers aside and ignoring God's call to biblical unity—and we'll continue to watch the fearsome downward spiral of society. Or we can allow God's Spirit free reign in the deepest recesses of our hearts, cooperating with Him as He works a miracle of unity in His church—and witness a culture transformed by the love of Christ. Anything less is a cheap gospel that will yield only thorns. God is calling us out, men. Will we accept His invitation?

The Broken Lamb of God?

Have you ever wondered why the Holy Spirit took the form of a dove at Jesus' baptism? Why not an eagle or a hawk? I believe it's because a dove, more than any other bird, represents the meekness and gentleness of our Savior. Jesus is likewise depicted as a lamb, gentle and meek, humbled and broken—a lamb who submitted Himself willingly to the shearer's clippers. This is the key to everything we need to know about our walk with Jesus Christ. The One who destroyed forever the bonds of death "did not consider equality with God something to be grasped, but made himself *nothing*, taking the very nature of a servant, being made in human likeness. And being found in appearance as a man, he humbled himself and became obedient to death—even *death on a cross!"* (Phil. 2:6-8, emphasis added).

Our Lord willingly took the form of a servant and gave Himself over to a humiliating death on a cross in order that we might be reconciled to a holy God. Jesus Christ, our *Savior,* our *Rock,* the *Prince of Peace,* emptied Himself of His glory and shed His robe of majesty. He became a lamb and won us our freedom.

Is Jesus our standard? He revealed the cost of discipleship. Do we seek unity in the Body? Then we must accept His yoke of servanthood. Do we long to be rooted and built up in Him? Then we must become as meek as doves or lambs, surrender our pride, and let Him live and reign in its place. We must be broken, emptied, stripped of self, and cleansed of everything we harbor in our hearts that keeps us from a holy, righteous God.

What Does It Mean to Be Broken?

Being broken by God is the key to everything! But you may ask, what does it mean to be broken? The apostle Paul gave us the definition: "Godly sorrow brings repentance that leads to salvation and leaves no regret, but worldly sorrow brings death. See what this godly sorrow has produced in you: what earnestness, what eagerness to clear yourselves, what indignation, what alarm, what longing, what concern, what readiness to see justice done" (2 Cor. 7:10-11). A heart broken by "godly sorrow" is beautiful in God's sight. Such a heart is indignant to pride, repentant of sin, and undone by its own depravity. Such a heart is earnest and eager to see justice done. Jesus told us, "My grace is sufficient for you, for my power is made perfect in weakness" (2 Cor. 12:9). *Brokenness* is God's prerequisite for the release of His power. God pours out His Spirit in fullness as we're emptied and broken. That happens as we behold Christ crucified deep in our spirits, when we're so transfixed by His pain and sacrifice that we can't take our eyes off Him.

Oh, Lord Jesus, remove the scales from our eyes. Help us to see that You died for us. Help us to see how You love us! You paid the greatest price, sold it all for us. We were dead in our sins, separated from the Father and unable to share in His perfect love. But You came and died and brought us new life with the Father.

Pride, Judgment, Selfishness

On another of my recent trips to visit clergy, I went with some PK field staff to Boston, where we were to meet with about 17 pastors. Shortly after the meeting began, I felt the Lord's prompting. Stopping the discussion in midsentence, I asked every guy in the room if he would go to his knees and cry out to the Lord. "Let's ask God to break our hearts and empty us of our selfish desires," I said. "Let's ask God to fill our hearts with the Holy Spirit."

I didn't know what to expect. But moments later, one pastor raised his hand and said, "I can't do that. I've been preaching for 20 years, and frankly, I'm skeptical." That word *skeptical* went right through me. I saw his statement as pride, which comes by comparing oneself with another.

Another man stood up. "I can't do that either," he said. "There are people out there I can't *trust*." As he sat down, I saw judgment in his eyes.

A third raised his hand. "I appreciate that Promise Keepers has finally seen the pain pastors are in. I like that you honor clergy at your conferences. But as for what you're asking me to do, I can't do that." That struck me as *selfishness*.

Finally, a fourth pastor, an older black man, stood. In a soft, trembling voice, he said, "I came here angry. But right now I can't see past the depravity of my own heart. I can't see *anyone* else, only that my heart isn't right."

The meeting ended abruptly and inconclusively. I am convinced that if men would only allow themselves to be broken, God is red hot, on fire, and ready to move—but man's pride, judgment, and selfishness quench the Spirit's fire.

In Boston, God illustrated how those sinful attitudes are the enemy's most effective weapons, keeping men puffed up, alienated from Him and from one another. Everywhere we went, we encountered the same thing: Only one in four men was willing to kneel and pray a simple prayer of brokenness before God. *One in four.*

The Nine Qualities of a Disciple
John Wesley once said, "Give me 100 men who love God and hate sin, and we'll shake the gates of hell." That defiant statement was made by a broken man *about* broken men. In one short sentence, Wesley spelled out the job description of a disciple—in love with God, broken by sin, and empowered by God's Spirit to take on hell itself. Brokenness is a fundamental, nonnegotiable prerequisite for all God is calling us to do. I believe the Bible tells us there are at least nine traits of a man who has truly been broken. These are imperative qualities for anyone who wants to reflect the image of Jesus to

a world desperately needing to see Him. As you read each item, ask God to reveal where your own strengths and weaknesses lie.

1. A true disciple's love for God must be the greatest single consuming passion of his heart. Jesus said, "Anyone who loves his father or mother more than me is not worthy of me; anyone who loves his son or daughter more than me is not worthy of me" (Matt. 10:37). There's no mistaking it: We were created to be in a love affair with Jesus. Unrestrained love explains Abraham's willingness to sacrifice his son and why Abraham's faith was credited to him as righteousness (see Rom. 4:3). You might say, "I couldn't do that." Then you've disqualified yourself as a disciple of Jesus Christ. Your love for the Lord is not authentic. Scripture tells us the *only* way to please God is to be passionately in love with Jesus Christ. It's also the only way life makes sense.

If an objective observer looked closely at your life—the way you use your time, your energy, your talents, your money—what would he conclude about your level of love for God?

2. Jesus must come before self. Jesus said, "If anyone would come after me, he must deny himself and take up his cross daily and follow me" (Luke 9:23). When you're deeply in love, you hold back nothing. Jesus held nothing back and "for the joy set before him endured the cross, scorning its shame, and sat down at the right hand of the throne of God" (Heb. 12:2). Jesus knew the incomparable joy of being with the Father. Therefore, no fear or threat of death could intimidate Him. Knowing the inexpressible joy that awaited Him, He was able to give all.

I find it confusing when Christians continually question their calling or purpose. It tells me they're not really in love with Jesus. Psalm 138:8 says, "The LORD will fulfill his purpose for me." If we're so in love with Jesus that nothing else matters, we'll know our purpose. Jesus said eye has not seen nor ear heard what He has prepared for those who love Him; and all things work out for the good for those who love God. There's *nothing* He won't do for those who are passionately, wholeheartedly in love with Him.

On your list of priorities, where does Jesus fit?

3. A disciple must put Jesus before all things. The Lord warned His disciples, "In the same way, any of you who does not give up everything he has cannot be my disciple" (Luke 14:33). Our love relationship with Jesus isn't a give-and-take proposition in which we sacrifice some things and hold tightly to others. It's *everything.* Our love for Jesus has to be so real, so perfect, so strong, that everything else pales in comparison. We must be willing to surrender everything and "consider everything a loss compared to the surpassing greatness of knowing Christ Jesus" (Phil. 3:8). We must continually remind one another, "The earth is the LORD's, and everything in it" (Ps. 24:1). No *thing* is ours to hold onto.

Do you own anything you'd find it hard to give up if God asked you to?

4. *A disciple must be a man of biblical unity.* Jesus said, "I pray . . . that all of them may be one, Father, just as you are in me and I am in you" (John 17:20-21). When we're completely, genuinely caught up in our love of Jesus, our hearts are linked by His kindred Spirit. We're *family*; we care about one another; we don't sin against one another. Out of our mutual love for Him, we love one another so much that we would never step over each other to get what we want. If our love for Jesus so dominated our lives, we would truly be "one body and one Spirit . . . called to one hope . . . one Lord, one faith, one baptism; one God and Father of all" (Eph. 4:4-6).

When you think of other Christians who are different from you in some way, do you focus on the ties that bind or the differences that divide?

5. *A disciple must be obedient.* Jesus said, "Whoever has my commands and obeys them, he is the one who loves me" (John 14:21). Isaiah told God, "Here am I. Send me" (Isa. 6:8). This must become the burning desire of our lives— to be so committed to Jesus that we're constantly asking, "Lord, what do You want me to do? Tell me and I'll do it."

How quick are you to obey God's orders?

6. *A disciple has a world view.* Jesus told His disciples, "Therefore go and make disciples of all nations, baptizing them in the name of the Father and of the Son and of the Holy Spirit" (Matt. 28:19). Do we live and breathe to preach the gospel? Do we share God's heart for the lost? A disciple understands that obeying the Great Commission is not an option; it's an irrefutable command Jesus gives to each of His disciples.

Who in your family or workplace needs to be introduced to the Savior? How can you help make that introduction?

7. *A disciple loves the Word.* In this love relationship, we must always know what the Father is saying to us. But we can't hear His voice apart from His Word. Jesus said, "Man does not live on bread alone, but on every word that comes from the mouth of God" (Matt. 4:4). To become effective disciples,

we can't go for extended periods of time without reading and being nurtured, sustained, and equipped by God's holy Word. The more we feed ourselves with the Word, the more our love for it will grow.

What's your plan for spending time in the Word in the next weeks and months?

8. *A disciple has a love of prayer*. God is not a part-time God. He's there for anyone who seeks Him with all his heart, mind, and soul. Nothing draws us deeper into our love affair with God than earnest prayer. "But when you pray, go into your room, close the door and pray to your Father, who is unseen. Then your Father, who sees what is done in secret, will reward you" (Matt. 6:6). Prayer is God's gift to us. It's where He reveals a portion of His heart to us. But, amazingly, prayer is the most neglected discipline in the church today. Moses said, "If . . . you seek the LORD your God, you will find him if you look for him with all your heart and with all your soul" (Deut. 4:29). To experience God to the fullest, we must "pray continually; give thanks in all circumstances, for this is God's will for you in Christ Jesus" (1 Thess. 5:17-18).

How important is prayer to you?

9. *A disciple is empowered by the Holy Spirit*. "But you will receive power when the Holy Spirit comes on you; and you will be my witnesses . . . to the ends of the earth" (Acts 1:8). A disciple knows that his only source of power, discernment, and spiritual survival is the indwelling Spirit of God. A true disciple takes no pride or pleasure in his own wisdom or ability. He knows God alone is responsible for his good works.

What might Almighty God, working in and through you, be able to do in your home, church, and community in the coming years?

We Are Loved by God!

Men, everything I've tried to say in this chapter boils down to a simple statement: *Keep your eyes on the Savior!* If we avert them for an instant, we'll stray. God is calling us to His side, to know Him and to serve Him. He's calling us to raise the standard of Jesus Christ in our homes, our jobs, and our communities. But much more than that, He's asking us to keep our eyes fixed lovingly on His Son.

I cannot emphasize enough, *we are loved by God*. Oh, He loves us so much! In fact, He never sleeps for thinking about us. He never rests for watching over us, carefully attending to us. He is always reaching out and pulling for us. God has left nothing to chance. He is *never* not pulling for us. His love for you and me is all-consuming and unconditional. I repeat, Almighty God is *taken* by us. He's committed to us. Our Lord does not dangle His love before us or yank it away when we sin. He extends His love without reservation in all circumstances. He has given us purpose and significance in an intimate love relationship with Jesus Christ. *That's who He is.* We can trust a God who loves us like that.

Men, *this* is our purpose: To love God with all our hearts, minds, and strength. Only then will we be able to conduct ourselves in a manner worthy of Jesus Christ. Only when our love for Him is so all-consuming will we understand—and *obey*—His command to love our neighbors as ourselves. Under those circumstances, it would destroy us to deliberately sin against our brother or sister, because we know how much God loves that person, His *child*. We know how much it would hurt God. Then we'll stand firm in one spirit and contend for the faith. That's when Christ's church will become a force for healing in a lost world.

God is calling us to oneness of spirit, and oneness comes only through brokenness—the prerequisite for service to God. As we're broken, God will commission us and take us places we've never dreamed of. He'll use us to bring down racism and denominational divisions. But most importantly, He's calling us into a passionate, all-consuming love for Jesus Christ. We must be so secure in God's love for us, so united in our mutual love for Jesus, that nothing and no one we face in these next 25 years can possibly tear that relationship apart.

Lord, pierce our hearts as we pierced You with our transgressions. Reach deep into our hearts; turn our hearts of stone into hearts of flesh. Search our hearts, Lord, and remove any darkness, selfishness, judgment, or pride. Break us, Lord. Help us to know that Jesus is all we need. Don't let us walk away from You again. Don't let us walk away from one another. Let us love You so much that we would never deliberately sin against one another. We know You love us, Lord, but our hearts are cold. Break our hearts, and cause us to fall in love with You all over again.

The Barriers in Our Way

by
Gary J. Oliver

ill McCartney's challenge sounds great, doesn't it? Reading his chapter makes any red-blooded Christian man want to go out and sign up. Hundreds of thousands of men have already heeded the call. You, too, have stood up, signed up, and you're getting geared up. But 25 years from now, what will things look like? How many card-carrying Promise Keepers will there be?

Given who God is, what the Father has promised, what the Son provided by His death on the cross, and the power of the Holy Spirit, nothing can keep each of us from finishing well . . . except us.

Some guys are going to make it, some aren't. What will make the difference? A good way to answer that is to look at some of the things you can expect once you make the decision to be a lifelong promise keeper. And the best way to do that is for me to introduce you to a friend of mine.

Tim had been a Christian for several years. When he first asked Jesus to be his Savior, he was pumped. He wanted the world to know what Jesus had done for him.

When we first met a while later, he was still active in his church and committed to living a good life, but much of his passion had diminished. His love had grown cold. When I invited him to attend the 1993 PK conference in Boulder, he accepted immediately. He had heard about Promise Keepers and was curious to find out what this "men's thing" was all about.

"I wasn't ready for what happened to me," Tim said afterward. He was challenged by the speakers and moved by the sound of 50,000 men singing praises to Almighty God. "I felt God's hand. I experienced God's presence in a way I never had before." He wanted to do something about it. He knew he had to respond.

When Tim heard about the seven promises, he decided they were the qualities he wanted to define his character. Toward the end of the conference, he said, "I want to become a man of integrity. I want my life to count for Christ!" After a brief pause, he looked me in the eye and said, "Gary, would you agree to pray for me over the next six months?"

I could tell he was sincere, and I agreed to pray for him on the condition that he let me know regularly how things were going.

Tim agreed. "When I go home, my life is going to be different," he said with conviction. "I'm going to make some real changes. My wife, my kids, and my friends at work are going to see a new Tim." He had come as a promise seeker. He was leaving a promise maker. He was committed to becoming a promise keeper.

Due to our individual travel schedules and summer vacations, it was more than a month before I saw Tim again. "Tim," I said, "I kept my side of the agreement. I've been praying for you. How's it going?"

With a dejected look, Tim replied, "Well, Gary, it's a lot harder than I thought."

"Tell me about it," I responded.

Tim told a story I've heard from many men. I've experienced it numerous times myself. It's the story of a sincere commitment made in a moment of clear conviction, fueled by great enthusiasm and high expectations, only to be shattered by the reality of our humanity.

Tim's battle had started immediately. The voices of doubt and discouragement began to attack him right after the conference. You've probably heard some of these same comments in your own mind. I know I've heard them in mine.

Hey! What makes you think you can do this?

You've screwed up before, and you'll do it again.

This is just an emotional time. It will pass.

What happens if you don't pull it off? What will everybody think?

This spirituality isn't for ordinary guys. The guys who speak and write the books are a unique breed. This spiritual stuff comes easy for them.

"I could have handled the doubts," Tim said. "What really knocked me for a loop was how quickly I failed." He went on to describe how, in just the first month after his commitment, he had missed several quiet times, lost his temper and flipped off a driver who cut him off in traffic, forgot to attend one of his kids' conferences at school, and lost a battle with pornography. "Once again, I was a failure. Once again, I had blown it. Once again, I had made promises I didn't keep."

As Tim and I continued to talk, it became clear that his situation wasn't all that unusual. When he was done speaking, I smiled at him, reached out to shake his hand, and said, "Hey, big guy. Welcome to the club!"

When the surprised expression left his face, he asked, "What do you mean?"

I told him that his experience wasn't unique. In fact, it's common. "Tim, the barriers you've tripped over are similar to what all of us who want to become men of integrity face."

Toward the end of our time together, Tim asked if we could meet once a week for the next several weeks to discuss how to become a promise keeper. During our meetings, we opened the Bible and prayed for each other, and I told him about my own pilgrimage, the experiences of the men in my own accountability group, and the journey of thousands of men around the country with whom I've talked.

Why do some promise makers fail to become promise keepers? There are as many different barriers to becoming a godly man as there are men. But I've learned there are some common barriers Satan uses that significantly increase our vulnerability to setbacks and sin. The degree to which we're aware of and understand how to respond to the inevitable (and even necessary) disappointments and obstacles will be the degree to which we experience growth and maturity—and the degree to which we become promise keepers.

Barrier 1
We Forget Our True Identity

As Tim and I continued to meet, he would sometimes go through a long list of all his weaknesses and mistakes. He had become failure-focused. That's one of the core barriers we all face. Satan wants us to define ourselves by our weaknesses, to develop a failure focus rather than a faith focus.

I reminded Tim that when we look at our identity, it's critical that we start at the cross. If you've confessed your sins and asked Jesus to be your Savior, you've been born again. Because of His completed work on the cross, you have many strengths. Yet when you're in the midst of battle or you've fallen, you aren't likely to be aware of them. You're not likely to focus on who the Bible says you are in Jesus. But that's exactly what you must train yourself to do. What are some of those strengths? How's this for a start?

- We've been justified and are completely forgiven (see Rom. 5:1).
- We're free from condemnation (see Rom. 6:1-6; 8:1-4).
- We're the righteousness of God in Christ (see 2 Cor. 5:21) and are partakers of the divine nature (see 2 Pet. 1:4).
- We've received the Spirit of God into our lives (see 1 Cor. 2:12).
- We've been baptized into the Body of Christ (see 1 Cor. 12:13).
- We've been given the mind of Christ (see 1 Cor. 2:16).
- We have direct access to God through the Spirit (see Eph. 3:12).

God knows we're weak, that we'll make mistakes, that we aren't perfect. But as we align our perspective to His, we'll understand the process, be able to reach out for His hand, and get up and keep on growing.

Barrier 2
We Set Unrealistic Goals

From the beginning of his "new life," Tim was doomed to failure. In fact, he set himself up for it by making one of men's most common mistakes. Maybe it's related to our testosterone levels, or perhaps it's just the way we're raised. It doesn't matter what color we are, how much money we have, or how many degrees we've earned. We all tend to set unrealistic goals.

There's something masculine about doing the extreme, the outrageous, the impossible. If it's risky, if no one has ever done it before (and lived to tell about it), it's something for a "real man" to try. If it's small, it must be insignificant. If it's simple, it must be simplistic. In either case, it's not for a real man.

The summer Olympics in 1992 provided a great example of this myth. In anticipation of the Games, Reebok invested over $15 million in ads asking whether Dan O'Brien or Dave Johnson was the world's greatest decathlete.

They were considered a slam dunk to make the U.S. Olympic team and compete in Barcelona.

Everything went great until it came to the pole vault event at the U.S. Olympic Trials. The bar started at 14' 5-1/4". O'Brien had jumped this height and more hundreds of times. He could do it in his sleep. So rather than play it safe, he decided to pass at several lower heights before opening at 15' 9".

The athletic world was shocked when he failed on all three attempts to clear the bar. He went under it on his first and third attempts and knocked it off the supports while coming down on the second. If he had cleared the lowest of the lower vaults, even 14' 5-1/4", he would have earned enough points to finish second and make the Olympic team. But that was too easy. And because of his decision, he spent the 1992 Olympics in the broadcasting booth rather than on the field.

God wants us to dream great dreams and attempt great things. But He knows we need to do them one step at a time. When Israel took the Promised Land, they did it one city at a time. When I climb one of the Rocky Mountains here in Colorado, I do it one step at a time. And maturity in the Christian life comes one day, one step, one victory at a time.

Energized by the enthusiasm of 50,000 men, Tim thought he could come home and change years of bad habits in a matter of weeks. He had great intentions but unrealistic goals.

Near the end of our time together, I asked Tim to buy a can of Spam and bring it to our next meeting. When he stopped laughing and realized I was serious, he agreed.

"This little can of Spam is a great reminder of the key characteristics of good goals," I told him when we got together again. "Next time you talk to God about goals, think of this can and remember the word *SPAMO*." The S stands for "small and specific." The P stands for "practical." The A stands for "achievable." The M stands for "measurable." The O on the end stands for "observable." Good goals embody all five of these aspects.

When the explanation was over, I asked Tim, "How can you apply this to your life this week?"

He immediately responded, "In the area of my quiet time, I had decided to read the Word and pray 30 minutes a day."

I suggested, "How about if you start by setting your goal at 15 minutes a day five days a week? If you do more than that, great. But if you don't, you've still been successful."

Tim got the point. By the end of our time together, he had set SPAMO goals for three key areas in his life.

Let your long-range goals be big ones. God specializes in things people think are impossible. The Promise Keepers movement is a great example of that. But remember that when Moses crossed the Red Sea, he did it one step at a time.

Barrier 3
We Forget There Are No Little Things

One of the major lessons I've learned from my own failures is that there are no little things. That's why Christ said, "Whoever can be trusted with very little can also be trusted with much, and whoever is dishonest with very little will also be dishonest with much" (Luke 16:10). The majority of my failures haven't been major or catastrophic. Most were small and seemingly insignificant. Most often they didn't even involve outright sin, only laziness, poor judgment, or compromise.

But those seemingly little things set me up for, and made me more vulnerable to, other decisions that led me further off the "straight and narrow." The problem wasn't in my initial decisions but in the direction they took me and the perspective they robbed from me. A series of little five-degree changes can eventually lead to behaviors that will turn into failure.

Satan knows that if you're committed to being who God wants you to be, it will be hard to get you to do an about-face. But he can get you to veer off the road. Then he can talk you into taking what *seems* like a harmless detour. He can talk you into believing "it's not that bad." And he knows that if he can get you even slightly off course—if he can get you to take your eyes off our Lord or seduce you into believing you can do it on your own—*bingo*. He has won a major victory. That's why it's so important to cultivate the habit of being faithful in little things. If you do, you won't have to worry about the "much."

One launch of the space shuttle Challenger stands out in everyone's memory. It was unique. It was the first time ordinary citizens were allowed to participate in a NASA mission. But only 73 seconds into its flight, the spacecraft blew apart right before our eyes. And then we watched in horror as the trails of smoke and debris fell toward the ocean.

The cause of that tragedy revealed an even greater tragedy. The explosion could have been avoided. It was caused by poor judgment and flawed materials. A group of top managers failed to listen to the warnings of engineers down the line. They had been told of the questionable reliability of certain parts of the booster rocket, especially a rubber O-ring, under conditions of abnormal stress, such as below-freezing cold.

Those responsible for making the final decision were sure they knew best. They decided to go ahead with the launch. They were wrong. The ultimate conclusion is that the disaster was caused by the pride of being unwilling to consider little things.

Have you ever, like the NASA officials, ignored warnings when all seemed well? I have. My previous mistakes were God's warnings that I didn't heed. Looking back, it's clear that things had been deteriorating for some time, but I had grown less and less sensitive to the telltale signs. Although over the years there had been many clues that something was wrong, I hadn't "gotten the message" of my "minor" mistakes.

Barrier 3 is subtle, and that's what makes it so powerful. As a man who is seeking to "be conformed to the likeness of his Son" (Rom. 8:29), never forget that there are no little things.

Barrier 4
The Subtle Power of Temptation

Tim was shocked to discover that within a month of his commitment, he began to be tempted again in the area of pornography. "When I was in high school and college, I struggled with pornography," he said, "but it's been years since I've been tempted by that stuff."

Any of the men who have contributed to this book will tell you that temptation is one of the most powerful barriers Satan will put in your path. It doesn't matter how old you are, how smart you are, how long you've been a Christian, or how many Bible verses you've memorized. Temptation is one of the main weapons in Satan's arsenal against us.

Tim made a common mistake. He assumed that because he experienced temptation, he had failed. However, an occupational hazard of being a Christian is that you *will* be tempted. It isn't a sin. In fact, in some ways you should be encouraged when you experience temptation. As John Vianney stated, "The greatest of all evils is *not* to be tempted, because there are then grounds for believing that the devil looks upon us as his property."

Every person is vulnerable to temptation, because we still have some of the patterns of thinking and acting that we had before we were saved. After knowing Jesus, Peter still struggled with self-control, James and John still had anger problems, and Paul still wrestled with doing what he didn't want to do and not doing what he wanted to do.

No matter how strong you are spiritually, you'll still experience spiritual warfare. That's why Jesus warned His disciples to "watch and pray so that you will not fall into temptation. The spirit is willing, but the body is weak" (Matt. 26:41). As men committed to godliness, we must heed Peter's warning to "gird your minds for action." When we do that, we not only anticipate temptation, but we're also prepared for it. If we expect spiritual warfare and know we'll be tempted, we're much less likely to be caught off guard by a "sneak attack."

As David found when he was tempted by the bathing Bathsheba, the initial enticement is rarely to sin. It's more often a temptation to linger too long. And that becomes the first link in a chain of seemingly innocent choices that lead to destruction. From the clear teaching of Scripture, from my own experience, and from the stories of thousands of other men, I can tell you that *the longer you linger, the sooner you'll stumble*. Godly men are prompt to do God's will.

If we don't *immediately* identify tempting thoughts and take them captive to what we know to be true—if we don't *immediately* replace the wrong thinking with right thinking—we'll become so weak that we won't care what we do until *after* we've sinned and begun to taste the bitter consequences. If you want to know just how bitter the consequences of sin can be, read 2 Samuel 12.

With each rationalization, with each justification, we become weaker and weaker. Once we allow ourselves to entertain unhealthy thoughts, once we choose to compromise what we know to be true, the party is over. The battle has been lost.

God's demand for moral and sexual purity is clearly seen in passages like 1 Corinthians 6:18-20 and 1 Thessalonians 4:3-8. But once we understand the biblical absolutes, we need to go beyond that and determine what kinds of things are healthy and unhealthy. What one man can watch or listen to with no problem may open the door to unnecessary temptation for another man and increase his vulnerability to sin.

Every man needs to ask God to help him determine where the line between right and wrong is. In areas where God's will isn't clearly spelled out in Scripture, pray about it and seek the counsel of several wise friends. Once God has shown you where the line is, walk 10 yards back and make *that* your line! *Always* leave yourself a margin.

If God has told you not to go beyond the 50-yard line, don't tiptoe up to the 49-yard-two-feet-and-eleven-inch mark. Don't see how close you can get to the line without going over. That's about as smart as a scuba diver seeing how little air he can leave in his tank and still get to the surface. Expect temptation. Gird your mind for action. And don't walk too close to the line.

Barrier 5
We Underestimate How God Can Use Weakness

What kinds of things do we men usually boast about? That's right, our victories and accomplishments. What kinds of things do we deny or attempt to cover up? Right again! Our failures and weaknesses. But Paul said just the opposite: "If I must boast, I will boast of the things that show my weakness" (2 Cor. 11:30). Not only is it okay to have weaknesses, but he even boasted about his.

Now, either Paul wasn't smart or he knew something we don't. He had learned that God uses failure to give us a taste of our weakness and sinfulness. It's a reminder that we can be saved only by His mercy.

Like many of us, Tim was well aware of his weaknesses. That's why he was so depressed and felt like giving up. He didn't understand that God uses struggles to draw us closer to Himself. They force us to look down into the depth of our humanity and discover the deep-seated pockets of selfishness and pride we didn't know were there. In the process of growing in godliness, we learn that it's okay to admit weakness. In fact, it's more than okay. *It's absolutely essential.*

Jesus told Paul, "My grace is sufficient for you, for my power is made perfect in weakness." Thus Paul could say, "Therefore I will boast all the more gladly about my weaknesses, so that Christ's power may rest on me. That is why, for Christ's sake, I delight in weaknesses, in insults, in hardships, in persecutions, in difficulties. For when I am weak, then I am strong" (2 Cor. 12:9-10).

It's easy for our confidence to be based on our strengths, accomplishments, bank account, or résumé. But Paul's was based on God's faithfulness and love, His promises, and on what Jesus had accomplished for him at the cross.

At one of our breakfast meetings, I asked Tim, "Do you ever feel weak, powerless, discouraged, or frustrated?"

His immediate response was, "Yes!"

"Then" I replied, "you are prime material for God to use."

I went on to show him that time and again, the Bible tells us that God deliberately seeks out the weak things and the despised to do His work because

He can receive the greatest glory from them. And in my own more than 30 years as a Christian, I've come to see that God loves to build on our mistakes and failures. (I'm so convinced of this that I wrote an entire book about it, *How to Get It Right After You've Gotten It Wrong.*) He takes our weak wills, inadequate resources, inconsistent efforts, and imperfect vision and transforms them into the finest of building materials. Out of our helplessness and hopelessness, He is making something beautiful.

Barrier 6
The Desire to Quit!

Dan Jansen is a classic case of the power of determination and commitment. The world watched him through several Olympics. He's not the only person to have fallen on ice. Ice is slippery. In fact, one of the main reasons my boys like to go skating is to watch their dad fall. However, when you're a world-record-holding speed skater, you aren't supposed to fall, especially at the Olympics. But Dan Jansen fell—twice in the 1988 Olympics and again in the 1992 Games.

When the 1994 Olympics rolled around, Jansen announced this would be his last try for gold. Everyone thought that this time he would get his medal. The 500-meter race was a "sure thing." But 300 meters into the race, Jansen reached out to steady himself, and the momentary friction of his hand on the ice probably caused the 35 hundredths of a second's difference between the gold medal and his eighth-place finish.

When he stepped onto the Olympic ice again a few days later for the 1,000-meter race, Jansen was 0-for-6 in all Olympic races. He told his trainer he was feeling out of sorts. He knew his timing was off. He struggled for traction. Seven competitors had better times than his career best in the event. But this was going to be his last Olympic race, his last opportunity for a medal—his last chance to prove himself.

His odds didn't look good. But to the joy of millions of viewers, Dan Jansen won the 1,000 meters in world-record time. He had refused to give up. The obviously excited television announcer shouted, "Dan Jansen has seized the moment!"

Men, that's exactly what God is calling us to do. He wants us to "seize the moment." But it's so easy to get discouraged. There are so many voices telling us we can't do it. Others are better. We'll fail. You've heard those voices. So have I. That's why Paul reminded us, "Let us not become weary in doing good, for at the proper time we will reap a harvest if we do not give up" (Gal. 6: 9).

Growth and maturity take time. When we're first saved, it's common to experience a period of rapid growth. God knows we need to develop a strong root system. But that doesn't continue. God knows that if there's to be healthy, sustained growth, the pace must be modified.

A. H. Strong tells of a student who asked the president of his school whether he could take a shorter course than the one prescribed. "Oh, yes," replied the president, "but then it depends on what you want to be. When God wants to make an oak, He takes a hundred years, but when He wants to make a squash, He takes six months."

Dr. Strong also wisely noted that growth in the tree is not uniform. During a four-to-six-week period in May, June, and July, rapid growth occurs as woody fiber is deposited between the bark and the trunk. There may be more growth during this short period than in the rest of the year combined. But it's during the remainder of the year that solidification takes place. Without that process, the green timber would be useless (quoted in *Principles of Spiritual Growth,* pp. 12-13).

Philippians 1:6 tells us, "Being confident of this, that he who began a good work in you will carry it on to completion until the day of Christ Jesus." One of the important messages of this chapter is that God can cause all things to work together for good. In fact, if you understand the growth process, if you know there will be barriers, if you're willing to learn the lessons from failure, you're *more likely* to learn how to hurdle the barriers and turn them into opportunities. In God's hands, that's exactly what barriers become. And that's exactly what the evil one doesn't want you to know. *Hang in there. Don't quit!*

Barrier 7
The Fear of Failure

This last barrier is one of the most subtle and yet one of the worst. Almost all of us fear failure—fear making a commitment and not being able to keep it. Never forget, however, that an occupational hazard of being human is that we *will* make mistakes and we *will* fail. Cadavers never fail. They're calm, cool, and laid back. But they never accomplish anything, either.

In contrast, look at the apostle Paul. By the time he wrote the book of Romans, he had made two extensive missionary journeys. He had pioneered the Christian message throughout the eastern provinces of the Roman Empire. He had suffered repeated persecutions, made converts, discipled new believers, and established churches. We're not talking here about someone who just knew God's Word; the Holy Spirit used Paul to *write* Scripture.

So here we have this godly, wise, mature man, an all-star of the faith. Yet he wrote in Romans 7 that he still struggled and still blew it. Look at verses 15 through 25:

> I don't understand myself at all, for I really want to do what is right, but I can't. I do what I don't want to—what I hate. I know perfectly well that what I am doing is wrong, and my bad conscience proves that I agree with these laws I am breaking. But I can't help myself, because I'm no longer doing it. It is sin inside me that is stronger than I am that makes me do these evil things. I know I am rotten through and through so far as my old sinful nature is concerned. No matter which way I turn I can't make myself do right. I want to but I can't. When I want to do good, I don't; and when I try not to do wrong, I do it anyway. . . . It seems to be a fact of life that when I want to do what is right, I inevitably do what is wrong. I love to do God's will so far as my new nature is concerned; but there is something else deep within me, in my lower nature, that is at war with my mind and wins the fight and makes me a slave to the sin that is still within me. In my mind I want to be God's willing servant but instead I find myself still enslaved to sin. (*Living Bible*)

Several years later, an older, wiser, and even more mature Paul wrote to the believers in Philippi,

> I don't mean to say I am perfect. I haven't learned all I should even yet, but I keep working toward that day when I will finally be all that Christ saved me for and wants me to be. No, dear brothers, I am still not all I should be but I am bringing all my energies to bear on this one thing: Forgetting the past and looking forward to what lies ahead, I strain to reach the end of the race and receive the prize for which God is calling us up to heaven because of what Christ Jesus did for us. (Phil. 3:12-14, *Living Bible*)

Let's not kid ourselves. As long as we're alive, we'll struggle with the consequences of our sinful humanity. The only real question is, will we go through life reinventing the wheel, repeating the same failures over and over? Or will we stop, look, listen, and learn? One of the main characteristics distinguishing mature Christians from immature ones is that mature Christians learn!

Tim knew all about the fear of failure. He had spent many years as a prisoner of that fear, especially in the Christian life. But his new understanding of God's Word; of the power of little things; the SPAMO perspective on goal setting; the memory of 50,000 promise makers lifting their hearts and voices in praise to the living God—all these gave him a new and realistic hope.

The Road to Maturity

Recently, one of my friends told me about his golf game. "I've played golf for 20 years," he said. "I love the game, and I play several times a week. But over the years, I've developed some bad habits." To deal with those, he decided to take lessons from one of the top pros in Denver.

"I couldn't believe how difficult it was to change a few simple aspects of my game," my friend continued. "Unlearning unhealthy and automatic ways of swinging my club was a lot more work than I had thought." He had to spend hours working on new techniques. "At first I felt kind of silly doing some of the exercises he made me do. And after the first few practices, my arms ached." I could tell by how he talked that it really had been painful. "But now," he concluded with a smile, "it doesn't hurt me at all." His smile got even bigger, and with a tone of pride he added, "And I've lowered my handicap by six strokes."

I don't golf, but I'm told that dropping your handicap by six strokes is a major accomplishment. How was he able to improve bad habits he had practiced for over 20 years? His desire to grow, to progress, made him willing to risk pain, looking awkward, confronting feelings of inadequacy, and the challenge of change. He took the risk, paid the price, and won.

What's your goal? Is it to become what you want, what you think society wants, or what you think others want? Or is it to become the man *God* wants you to be? Once you understand how difficult the growth process can be, you won't be caught off guard by the inevitable barriers you'll face. You won't be surprised by the setbacks all of us experience. As you develop a biblical view of who you are in Christ—when your significance and security are based on His completed work for you on the cross and not on your performance or some perceived need to be right all the time—you'll be more open to healthy change. You'll want to learn and grow to become more of who God would have you to be.

What Bill said in the first chapter about the potential impact of a million Christlike men is true. It's possible. It can happen. But maturity doesn't come automatically or overnight. Becoming a godly man takes time and involves a battle.

Conclusion

As we come to the end of this chapter, you face a choice. It's the same choice that Tim faced and that I face. God wants us to grow, to become like our Lord Jesus Christ. But growth involves change—doing something different. And that means being willing to move out of your comfort zone.

When we understand the barriers to expect and the vital role failure plays in the growth process, however, it becomes much easier for us to take the risks that can result in growth. Remember that the One who saved you is the same One who . . .

- can keep you from stumbling;
- can cause all things to work together for good;
- can supply all your needs; and
- will never give you more than you can handle.

Not only *can* He do those things, but He *must* if we're to overcome the barriers and grow more like Jesus. Never forget that *we can't do it alone*—we can only do it with His help. Jesus said, "Remain in me, and I will remain in you. No branch can bear fruit by itself; it must remain in the vine. Neither can you bear fruit unless you remain in me. . . . [A]part from me you can do nothing" (John 15:4-5).

Only as we prayerfully, humbly submit ourselves to God, seeking His wisdom, direction, and strength day by day, will we mature in our faith and increasingly reflect the nature of His Son. By His grace, He will do that for us through His indwelling Spirit. In fact, He wants that for us more than anything and is just waiting for our willing cooperation.

Are you willing? Then let's take our first look in the next chapter at a planning process that can help us get in step with what the Spirit may want to do in our lives.

Closing the Gap

by
John Trent

t's my privilege to introduce to you a personal change process that runs
throughout this book. As you work through each chapter, you'll discover
it's a prayerful method to help you become more like Jesus Christ. It's a way
of facing and making immediate *and* long-term changes that can help you
stand strong in moral purity and reflect a God-honoring love to those around
you. That includes a deeper love for your family and for a lost world as well.

Creating your own prayed-over plan of action can be a powerful tool for
breaking down racial walls and barriers. It will encourage you to be an active
churchman, supporting your pastor and mentoring others. In short, it's a how-
to manual for applying the seven promises of a Promise Keeper. The goal of
this program isn't to define the promises for you, nor to show you how other
men have lived them out to the glory of God. Rather, here's *your* chance
to get into the game and turn these principles into everyday habits and attitudes that can increase your love for the Savior and others.

That's quite a challenge, we know, but it's also why we feel so strongly that
this is one of the most important books yet from Promise Keepers. The process
you'll learn in this book is called "Closing the Gap." It's an active method of
evaluating where you are today in your walk with Jesus, prayerfully deciding

31

where you'd like to be in three years, then making plans for how you can get there with God's enabling grace and help. Along the way, you'll be challenged to confront inevitable barriers and live out God's infallible, unfailing Word.

While all that may sound complicated, we've broken down this life-change process into a series of understandable steps and cycles. In addition, we've provided a number of practical, "hands-on" experiences and tools to weave biblical principles into your everyday life.

With the aid of a small group of friends (and, when appropriate, with your spouse if you're married), you'll create a personal plan of action that remains flexible to God's leading, encourages loving accountability, and stays strategically targeted toward your particular goals and setting over time. And far from being presumptive of God's will for your life (or chaining you to a legalistic way of living), it can free you to become more like Jesus as you walk worthy of the high calling you've received.

By now, you've read Randy Phillips's challenge to go the distance and Bill McCartney's important call to brokenness (the starting point for *any* genuine change). After reading Gary Oliver's chapter, you're also aware of the barriers to putting any commitment to spiritual growth into action. Now let's look at the Closing the Gap process itself.

The process begins with an important reflective exercise that helps put God's leading in your life in historical context. After taking that positive step back, we'll step forward and look at each of the seven promises in a specific, applicational way. This includes reading the insights of leading men of faith, who discuss the keys they've found to putting the seven promises into everyday practice. Then you'll be encouraged to personally:

- Create worksheets for all seven promises and later combine them into a workable, long-term plan of action.
- Initiate a couple of "growth cycles" that consistently reinforce your goals and help you confront negative barriers.
- Receive a challenge to take what you've learned and mentor other men in the future.

The process you'll learn focuses on long-term change, not quick fixes or emotional commitments easily forgotten. So if you're ready to take the first step in a lifelong distance race, read on as we talk about the biblical basics behind this process and then look at a "highlight film" of the Closing the Gap plan of action.

Building on Biblical Bedrock

Two key verses set a foundation for this process. The first affirms that God *has* positive plans for your life: "'For I know the plans I have for you,' declares the LORD, 'plans to prosper you and not to harm you, plans to give you hope and a future'" (Jer. 29:11). The second verse speaks of our having God's strength to fully live out that plan: "For God did not give us a spirit of timidity, but a spirit of power, of love and of self-discipline" (2 Tim. 1:7).

Far from being lost, hopeless, or helpless, we have a hopeful future because of what Jesus has done. What's more, as believers, we can appropriate God's power, love, and discipline to make daily steps toward His best for our lives! It's that positive view of our potential and power in Jesus that surrounds the Closing the Gap process.

What do we mean by "closing the gap"? As you'll see in detail in the pages to come, it's a reference to taking stock of where we are today in our walk of faith and comparing that to where we would like to be three years from now (and beyond) if we were fully living for Christ. Narrowing that "gap" between where we are today and the Christlikeness we'd like to reflect is the goal of this whole process.

The Goal of the Closing the Gap Process
The goal is to recognize God has a positive plan for your life and to appropriate His power, love, and discipline to move toward it.

The Closing the Gap plan you'll create is something unique to you. *However, we strongly encourage you to develop it in the supportive atmosphere of a small group, and with input and encouragement from your spouse if you're married.*

Can you work through this process alone? Yes. But doing so would be like watching the Super Bowl alone on a fuzzy, six-inch, black-and-white, hand-held television compared to joining with a group of close, cheering friends who have a 10-foot color projection screen! You can get the basic picture by yourself, but you'll miss a lot of color, contrast, and intensity. On a more serious note, while you can go into battle alone, we wouldn't recommend it. We *strongly* believe you'll gain far more in terms of encouragement, loving accountability, objectivity, and shared biblical insight to "go the distance" if you're a part of a small group.

We'll talk more about the benefits of being in a small group, and even how to begin one, in chapter 4. But for the purpose of our overview, we'll assume you've taken the faith-stretching step of inviting two or three friends to join you in enriching each other's lives.

Overview of the Closing the Gap Process

A. Before You Walk Through Each Promise Area . . .

1. Recognize that real change begins with a spirit of brokenness. The Closing the Gap process begins with the biblical truth Bill McCartney stated in chapter 1. Namely, being broken and humble before the Lord is the *only* basis for genuine change. God opposes the proud, yet He gives grace to the humble (James 4:6). Being open to counsel and correction and recognizing our complete reliance on His forgiveness, love, and strength is a key to growth. The first step we need to take if we're serious about growing in Christlikeness is to bow before Him.

2. Realize you have a sworn enemy when it comes to making personal and spiritual changes. As we've seen in Gary Oliver's chapter, you not only face personal barriers to change, but you also have a determined enemy of your soul. Satan tricked Adam and Eve and tested the Lord Jesus, and he would like nothing better than for you to forget any "foolish" ideas about totally committing your life to Jesus. Learning to expect and confront personal and spiritual challenges, both from within and from without, is another important aspect of this process of long-term spiritual growth.

3. When we say this is a "prayerful" process, we mean it! As you work through the individual evaluation sheets after each chapter and each of the different cycles we'll present, you'll notice an emphasis on prayer. That isn't because it's a nice, optional extra. It's an absolute essential. We've built in specific times of prayer both individually and as a group for you to go boldly before God's throne, laying out your strengths, weaknesses, hopes, fears, and goals. If anything positive comes from this planning process, we're convinced it will be through God's power and Spirit, spoken to us through His Word, and spoken to Him in prayer.

B. Developing Your Plan, Promise by Promise

The next several pages will give you an overview of the change process and individual tools you'll be using in chapters 4-11. This is only an introduction to familiarize you with the worksheets and terminology we'll use. We'll go into more detail on each worksheet and aspect of this plan in the chapters that follow.

1. Begin to move forward by briefly looking back. The first exercise you'll do with your group of supportive friends is to share your "Personal History" sheet. I'll explain further in chapter 4 how to fill out this form, and I'll provide several scriptural examples to show how to use this information in a positive way. For example, the completed sheet below captures the life of a man named "Joe."

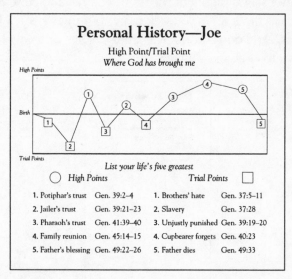

As you've probably guessed, the Joe represented above is none other than Joseph in the Old Testament, the hated younger brother who ended up saving his older brothers' lives. And as you can see from his graph, Joseph's challenging walk of faith is reflected in five "high points" and five "trial points" that significantly affected his life.

An important prerequisite to closing the gap on Christlikeness is to recognize God's presence in the highs and lows of our lives. The Personal History sheet is not only a good way to look back and see God's presence and leading in each decade of your life, but it will also help you identify and face repeating patterns. Additionally, as a small-group tool, it can quickly give your friends important insights into your history, as well as serve as a "prayer guide" for them.

2. Next, read each promise area and complete the forms that follow. Read the main body of each chapter (chaps. 5-11). Outstanding Christian leaders have written on each of the seven promises. As you read their material, you may be surprised to find they've struggled in areas just like you, and you'll certainly be encouraged to see how they've appropriated God's power to keep their promises.

After reading about each promise, your first task in planning to close the gap is to choose a "personal evaluation point" for that promise. This will help you identify where you are today on a "1 to 10" scale, provide a baseline for future evaluations, and highlight the "gap" you need to close over the next three years (and a lifetime) as you seek to live out this aspect of Jesus' life and love for others. And don't worry: Regardless of age or level of maturity, *all* of us have gaps to close in every area.

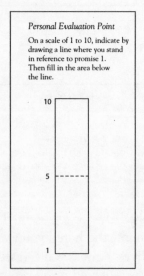

Personal Evaluation Point

On a scale of 1 to 10, indicate by drawing a line where you stand in reference to promise 1. Then fill in the area below the line.

10

5

1

Next, you'll be challenged to set a personal "horizon." (For our purposes in this book, we're setting the horizon at three years from now.) This is a "hands-on" form where you'll develop a written description of the man you're asking God to help you become in the long term in this promise area. As you fill out your horizon sheet, you'll be encouraged to pray, reflect, dream, identify barriers, and seek counsel if needed.

```
Setting a Prayerful Horizon

Lord willing, 3 years from now
my life will reflect this promise
in these ways:

  My age today          _____
  3 years from today  _____

  _____
  _____
  _____
  _____
  _____
  _____
  _____
  _____
  _____
  _____
  _____
  _____
  _____
  _____
```

3. Develop a specific plan of action to reach your personal horizon. Once you've shared your Personal History form, completed your personal evaluation form, and set your prayerful horizon, you've got the basic building blocks to shape a personalized, God-honoring plan for long-term growth. With your past, present, and prayerful future laid out before you, you'll then develop specific "action points." In fact, you'll come up with three action points, each matched with a potential barrier you may have to overcome, for each promise area. These specific actions and attitudes form the daily "how to's" as you close the gap toward Christlikeness.

```
                    Action Plan Worksheet

            Knowing that I need to improve in this commitment,
            I will do my best to take a step of growth by following
            through in the three areas listed below:

1. Action Point
   _____
   _____
   Potential Barrier
   _____
   _____
2. Action Point
   _____
   _____
   Potential Barrier
   _____
   _____
3. Action Point
   _____
   _____
   Potential Barrier
   _____
   _____
```

While each man in your group will come up with his own plan, he's not alone in implementing it. That's why you'll next be asked to list a specific accountability time and individual(s) who will help you follow through on your action steps and confront any barriers.

> **Accountability Commitment**
> Who _____
> When _____

C. Synthesize an Overall Plan of Action

After working through and developing a growth plan for each promise over the course of seven weeks, in chapter 12 you'll combine all seven evaluations and action-plan sheets into a single descriptive overview. Here you'll take the personal evaluation point from each promise and put them all on a "Life Perspective" sheet. That will let you see at a glance where your life is in regard to the seven promises and which gaps are the widest between where you are and where you want to be. Here's a sample completed sheet:

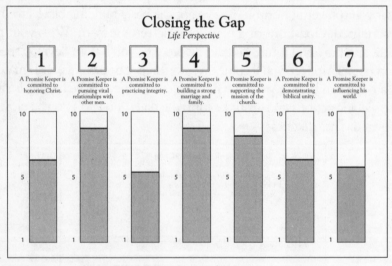

D. Begin to Live Out Your Plan

After creating your evaluation and action plan, your focus switches to application as you and your group "cycle" through several seven-week growth experiences. We'll go into detail on these cycles in chapter 12, but a key part of making this plan a flexible, life-changing tool is having your small-group meeting center on these growth cycles. *What are they?*

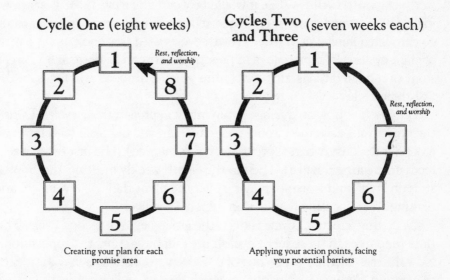

Cycle One (eight weeks)

Cycles Two (seven weeks each) and Three

Rest, reflection, and worship

Rest, reflection, and worship

Creating your plan for each promise area

Applying your action points, facing your potential barriers

Throughout Scripture, we find a consistent pattern of work and then rest, work and then rest. For example, God followed that pattern in the book of Genesis, when He created the world and instituted the Sabbath. He directed His people to follow the same pattern. They were to do this by tilling the soil for seven years, then allowing the land to "rest." *A growth cycle is an opportunity to do something similar in a world that has all but forgotten what it means to "rest in the Lord."*

During the first seven weeks of your study, it will take work and reflection to go through each promise area and come up with a personal plan. But on the eighth week, when your plan is complete, you and your group will use your meeting time to pray, worship, and "rest." You'll reflect, refine and prioritize your plans, and pray that God would enable you to live them out to His glory and the benefit of your families and world.

The idea of cycling through a core set of principles isn't new. For example, Ben Franklin, one of America's founding fathers, applied this approach to a set of core values he admired. As a young man of 22, he identified 13 "virtues" he wanted to reflect throughout his life. He then focused on one virtue a week for 13 weeks, after which he would start the process all over again. At the age of 78, he remarked that while he hadn't "laid hold" of perfection in any area, he was "far the better man" for having tried to live them out.

Don't worry! We don't expect you to stay in your small group for 56 years'

worth of growth cycles! While it would be wonderful to spend 50 years growing old with several committed Christian friends, we recommend your group
go through a *minimum* of three growth cycles with this book, up to a total
of eight cycles. (In short, the plan presented here can be done as a 22-week
study or modified to last up to an entire year.) This book will focus on the
first three cycles.

Let's look at how an average group might approach these cycles. During
their first cycle, each man would create his plan and discuss it with his small
group (and spouse, when appropriate, if he's married). The first seven weeks
focus on creating the plan. Then in the eighth weekly meeting, the emphasis is on "rest" and worship, praying over the plans they've developed, and
revising and refocusing their action steps as God leads.

Once this "creative" cycle is over, the group begins a second cycle. This
time (and in each subsequent cycle), the emphasis shifts to "application."
Now the men identify which one of the seven promise areas they most need
to work on. Perhaps it's the one in which they gave themselves the lowest
score, or it may be the one they feel is the most important at this time regardless of score. Also, each man might choose his own top-priority area individually, or the group might pick the area together so they will all be working
on the same promise at the same time.

Once the first area to concentrate on has been selected, the men will spend
two weeks focusing on each of their three action points and potential barriers for that promise. That's a total of six weeks devoted to making positive
changes in their lives to better fulfill that particular promise.

At the end of this second cycle, they would end with a seventh week of
"rest" and worship. This gives the group time to stop and reflect, readjust their
plans if necessary, thank God for what He's accomplished in their lives so far,
and pray for any individual who's facing a particularly trying barrier.

A group can stop after three cycles (eight weeks of creating their plan and
14 weeks of applying it to their top two promise areas). However, some groups
may want to continue this process of working and resting up to a *total* of eight
times in order to cover all seven promises. That's part of the flexibility of this
program that allows you to tailor it to the needs of you and your group.

End Your Group Experience with a New Beginning

After your group has completed its agreed-upon number of growth cycles,
we're challenging you to do something that may take you out of your comfort

zone but will also be a great experience. That's to take what you've learned here—*and begin a new group!*

As a "veteran" of this process, you may be ready to help another group of three to four men complete the same process you've been through.

"Wait a minute, Trent!" you say. "That sounds a lot like mentoring."

Very perceptive. That's exactly where we pray this experience will lead. Our goal is that you won't just learn and apply this process yourself (as beneficial as that may be), but that you will in turn teach this method of living out God's Word to other men, who in turn will teach it to other faithful men as well. In fact, you'll discover that it's in *teaching* this material that the learning process really begins!

This Sounds Like a Lot of Work!

We're asking you to do a lot of work at both creating and applying your plan. That's why we said at the beginning of this book that if you're going to close the gap on Christlikeness, you'll need to be a full-time player. But we're convinced that any time and energy you spend in living for Jesus will result in spiritual and relational rewards that can benefit your life, your family, and future generations as well.

If you're ready to gather a few good men and jump into this exciting process, the next chapter is where the action begins. But before you skip ahead, we would like to address four important questions many men have about this Closing the Gap process. Take a look and see if those questions and answers help you make a stronger, more enthusiastic commitment to the growth God wants to produce in you.

Four Important Questions

1. When We Talk About Change, What Do We Really Mean?

In a sentence, *change means a commitment to do things differently and the follow-through to make it happen.* In other words, we're not just talking about a change in perspective, but also about a change in what we value and believe that involves or even demands a change in our actions.

We've all seen men who attended Promise Keepers events and raised their voices in praise to God—only to go home and raise their voices in anger at their families. Maybe you're one of them. We can't do anything to change the past, but we *can* do something about the choices we make today and tomorrow. To borrow a phrase from the apostle James, we can go from simply being *hearers* of the Word to being *doers* of the Word.

That's what God calls us to, men. When we encounter Him, it should change us. *And that means a difference in what we believe and the way we live.*

Keep one important thing in mind as you begin this study. If you're married, your spouse may not be impressed with your words, "Honey, I'm getting a plan, and I'm really going to make some consistent changes this time." She's waiting for your actions. If you've broken your promises to your children a hundred times because of business priorities, don't expect a "That's wonderful, Dad! You're in a small group!" But do expect them to test your words against your actions.

2. Is It Really True That Anyone Can Change?

Absolutely! To say there's someone out there who's beyond change is like saying there's someone beyond the reach of God's forgiveness and power. May it never be! That's not to say all men *will* change, but if they don't, it's not for any lack of God's power. The Lord is able to make the most hardened sinner into a saint. Take the apostle Paul, for instance.

In a moment of quiet reflection, Paul wrote his friend in ministry Timothy and said, "Here is a trustworthy saying that deserves full acceptance: Christ Jesus came into the world to save sinners—*of whom I am the worst*" (1 Tim. 1:15, emphasis added). It's easy to think that was just Paul's brand of false modesty, but listen to how far his sin took him: "And when the blood of your [God's] martyr Stephen was shed, I stood there giving my approval and guarding the clothes of those who were killing him" (Acts 22:20).

It wasn't that Paul just happened to pass by as Stephen was being stoned, wondering what the commotion was about. He stood there and callously watched a group of overzealous countrymen kill an innocent man. And he didn't just look the other way until the "unfortunate incident" was over. His eyes were riveted on Stephen's blood-spattered body; his ears attuned to his cries of pain. He listened and looked with satisfaction as each rock found its mark and slowly pummeled the life out of someone guilty of nothing more than confessing Jesus as Lord. Stoning is a horrible way to die, and Paul watched with satisfaction as it happened. And if that wasn't enough, he took care of everyone's *coats* while they participated.

How do you feel about people who commit ruthless murder, like a convenience-store robber who forces the clerk to hand over the money and then shoots him or her in the head anyway? That was Paul. He was an arrogant, ruthless, cold-hearted murderer—a self-proclaimed "protector" of God's law— the kind of man you bow to as he approaches and spit at after he passes by.

Was Paul a sinner? There was none worse. Did he need to change? No question. And on his way to Damascus one day, he had an encounter with Someone who radically altered his life. Broken over his sin and transformed by God's Spirit, Paul turned from a life of hardness and cruelty to one of compassion and Christlikeness. Thinking back over that experience, he told Timothy, "But for that very reason I was shown mercy so that in me, the worst of sinners, Christ Jesus might display his unlimited patience *as an example for those who would believe on him* and receive eternal life" (1 Tim. 1:16, emphasis added).

God changed *him*.

He can change *you*.

3. Given That God's Will Is Unchangeable, Isn't It Presumptuous to Make a Plan for My Life?

That's an important question, particularly because of the emphasis the authors of this book place on developing a personal, prayerful plan of action. In a word, the answer is no. Even Jesus acknowledged that making plans is a normal and necessary part of life (see Luke 14:31). Nehemiah, no doubt, had to plan carefully for the completion of Jerusalem's walls. And Proverbs 21:5 commends planning when it says, "The plans of the diligent lead to profit."

So the issue isn't planning itself. It's our *perspective* that's important. Proverbs 16:9 says, "In his heart a man plans his course, but the LORD determines his steps." In other words, we can and should make plans in many areas of life. But the balance comes in realizing that God is in control, it's His plan, and it's His Word we're seeking to live out.

That's why James warned the readers of his epistle, "Now listen, you who say, 'Today or tomorrow we will go to this or that city, spend a year there, carry on business and make money.' Why, you do not even know what will happen tomorrow. . . . Instead, you ought to say, *'If it is the Lord's will*, we will live and do this or that'" (James 4:13-15, emphasis added).

All this means we need to hold our plans, including our Closing the Gap plans, loosely. One of my favorite professors in seminary, Dr. Howard Hendricks, used to kid us about people in ministry who come up with grandiose plans, take them to the Lord, and say, "Here's my plan, Lord. Now bless it!"

James didn't pull any punches when he told us that kind of attitude is arrogant (see 4:16). Instead, as we seek to get some specific goals woven into our plan, we need to approach Him and say, "Lord, this is what I'd like to do to move closer to You. From everything I can see and what I know of your Word, it looks like a good plan. But if You want to change it, rearrange it, or scrap it all together, I acknowledge You have every right. And by the way . . . if You do change it, I won't complain."

That can be scary until we realize God's sovereign control should give us great security. As mentioned earlier, He Himself has said, "'For I know the plans I have for you,' declares the LORD, 'plans to prosper you and not to harm you, plans to give you hope and a future'" (Jer. 29:11).

That promise holds just as true for those of us living on this side of the Cross. Paul reminded the Ephesians that we've received God's mercy "in order that in the coming ages he might show the incomparable riches of his grace, expressed in his kindness to us in Christ Jesus" (Eph. 2:7).

So when God alters our plans, He's simply redesigning the situation so that we see His grace in new and exciting ways.

We've said it before, but let's say it again: There's a prayerful flexibility built into the planning process provided in this book. God alone holds the future in His hands, and He reveals it to us day by day. But as Martin Luther once said, "If I knew the world were to end tomorrow, I'd plant an acorn in my backyard today." It's important to have a plan, and it's just as important to leave it flexible to God's leading.

4. Will the Changes I Make Using This Plan Really Last?

For many men, previous plans of action have been nothing more substantial than a New Year's resolution like "I'll never eat another dessert!" But we believe that the support of a small group, coupled with the growth cycles you'll experience with that group of men, will give you strength for a marathon, not just a 50-yard dash. Take time to work through each promise area, and then read chapter 12 to see how these cycles provide a structure for accountability, redirection, renewal (through times of "rest"), and multiplication (through your becoming a mentor of another "Go the Distance" group).

Remember, too, that there are always new "miracle diet" books on the shelf because people forget the *real* "secret" to losing weight—*daily discipline*. Any man can walk away from any plan at any time. That's why Jesus taught us to pray about "daily bread" and the strength to face "daily trials." What we've sought to do in this Closing the Gap process is to give you tools, encouragement, and support to build daily disciplines. And God's Spirit within you can give you the faith and energy for truly long-term change.

Can you make lasting changes and become more like Jesus day by day for the rest of your life? Absolutely!

Moving Forward by Stepping Back

by
John Trent

For die-hard college football fans, it doesn't get any better than attending a national championship game . . . *unless you happen to get your tickets for free.* I'm not trying to incite a spirit of jealousy, but that's exactly what happened to my wife, Cindy, and me on January 2, 1996. There we sat at Sun Devil Stadium in Tempe, Arizona, with my board chairman and his wife.

Earlier that afternoon, he had called to ask if we wanted to go with them to *the* game. A few hours later, we were crammed into our seats amidst a sea of Nebraska Cornhusker fans, watching the pregame blimps, bands, and parachute jumpers.

As part of the opening festivities, highlight films of both teams' undefeated seasons were shown on the massive "Jumbo-Tron" screen that dominates the south end zone. With the kickoff just minutes away, thousands watched clips of spectacular scoring passes, bone-jarring sacks, and major league hits leading up to this game. Both the Nebraska fans and the Florida Gator backers were roaring for the game to start.

What does this story have to do with "going the distance"? In the introduction and opening chapter, you were challenged to join a multitude of men in "going the distance" with Jesus, and then you were reminded that the start-

47

ing line for such a life begins with being broken. Next you were shown common barriers you could expect to face in living for Him, and in the last chapter, you got an overview of the plan of action we'll follow.

In some ways, those chapters are like listening to a pregame "chalk talk." You've now heard directly from the "general manager" and "coach," been reminded of your opponent's strengths and strategies in the scouting report, and been shown a winning game plan. Now it's time to walk through the tunnel and run onto the field.

But just before you tee up the ball and get into the game with your small group, look up at the "Jumbo-Tron" screen. There you'll see a "highlight" film playing of your life story!

Moving Forward Begins with Seeing God in Your Past

The process of closing the gap between where you are today and where you want to be by God's grace begins with a brief, positive look back. That's because whether you've had nothing but "undefeated" seasons in your walk of faith or you've struggled just to stay in the game, it's important to see where God has brought you. It's vital for your small group as well.

As you begin your first growth cycle, we want to make sure you get to know those in your group at a *deeper-than-surface* level. To do that, it's important that each person fill out his Personal History sheet. You were introduced to this sheet in chapter 3 as a graphic way of capturing some of the strengths and struggles, the high points and difficult challenges, that have shaped your life story. And in the process of describing your personal history to your small group, we trust three things will take place.

First, we think you'll be surprised at what you learn about those in your group—even men you've known for years. That's because it's easy to think that being around someone is the same as really knowing him, and it isn't.

In the weeks to come, you may gain more from this small-group experience than you have from any group you've been in before. But that won't happen if the sharing level never gets deeper than exchanging "the weather report." ("How're you doing?" "Great! How're *you* doing?" "Great!") Filling out and discussing the following Personal History sheet is a great ice-breaker to communicate who you are and where God has taken you. In fact, it's one way of giving a "pictorial" testimony of how God brought you to Himself, which is one of the most encouraging things you can do.

As you describe your sheet, you might say, for instance, that a particular low point was the very thing God used to bring you to Himself (e.g., "We had a child who went through some difficult physical challenges, yet through that experience, we came to know Jesus"). For others, a high point may be the culmination of years of hard work or even the answer to years of prayer (e.g., "After 20 years of my wife praying for me, God finally broke down my pride and I went to church, where I came to know Jesus").

Second, as you think back over your life, you may be surprised to find patterns, both positive and negative, that have distinctly marked your past. The Gospel of John tells us, "You will know the truth, and the truth will set you free" (8:32). As you look at your "ups" and "downs," you may see behavioral trends that need to be exposed to God's truth. Discussing these with your small group can provide the accountability you need to continue positive patterns and confront negative ones.

Third, you'll find life patterns similar to yours in Scripture. After completing your Personal History sheet (see page 50), take a look at the three completed Personal History charts that follow. Then, after explaining your own chart to your group, discuss the answer to this question: Is your personal history most like that of a "Joseph," a "David," or a "Jonah"?

The "Joseph" Pattern: Consistent Spiritual Growth

Here's the graph of the patriarch Joseph's life we gave you in chapter 3:

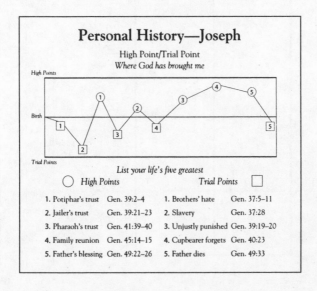

Personal History

High Point/Trial Point
Where God has brought me

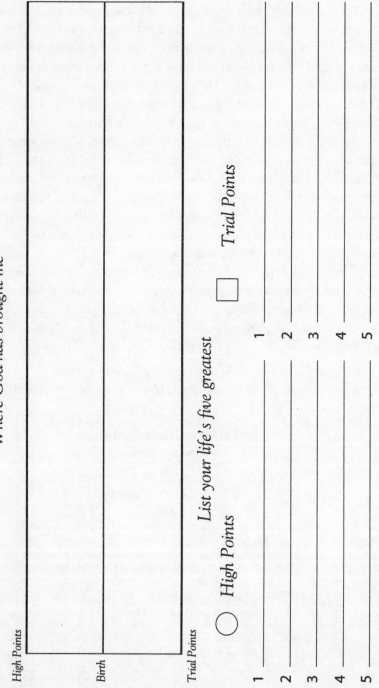

List your life's five greatest

○ High Points

□ Trial Points

High Points

1
2
3
4
5

Trial Points

1
2
3
4
5

Look closely at Joseph's high points and trial points. Outside of the Lord Jesus Himself, perhaps no person in Scripture demonstrated as many Christlike traits. He was tempted to sin by Potiphar's wife (as Jesus was tempted by Satan), yet he chose to resist and flee. Joseph could have condemned those who sought to take his life (his brothers), but like Jesus, he chose to forgive them. In fact, throughout his life we see a pattern of consistent spiritual trust and growth. His life was so focused on God that the lowest points he faced were caused by living in a fallen world, not his own sin.

Perhaps you've grown up knowing Jesus and matured steadily in Him throughout your life. *That's great!* Not that you're perfect in any way, nor that you've had as many dramatic opportunities to trust God as Joseph did. But an overall look at your life story reflects a consistency of spiritual growth, and most of the trials you've faced have come from living in a fallen world instead of from falling yourself.

If that generally describes your life, after explaining your Personal History sheet to your small group, tell them you're in the Joseph category.

The David Pattern: An Up-and-Down Spiritual Experience

As you look at this second great man of faith's Personal History sheet, notice the difference between the highs and lows in David's life compared to Joseph's.

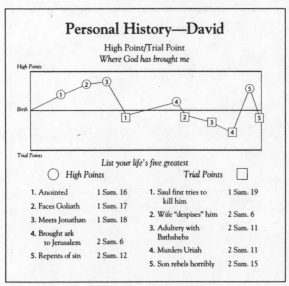

Personal History—David

High Point/Trial Point
Where God has brought me

List your life's five greatest

○ High Points		Trial Points ☐	
1. Anointed	1 Sam. 16	1. Saul first tries to kill him	1 Sam. 19
2. Faces Goliath	1 Sam. 17	2. Wife "despises" him	2 Sam. 6
3. Meets Jonathan	1 Sam. 18	3. Adultery with Bathsheba	2 Sam. 11
4. Brought ark to Jerusalem	2 Sam. 6	4. Murders Uriah	2 Sam. 11
5. Repents of sin	2 Sam. 12	5. Son rebels horribly	2 Sam. 15

In many ways, David's life of faith looks like an EKG readout! You see high highs, like his great victories of faith in defeating Goliath and bringing the ark back to Jerusalem. Yet you also see deep, dramatic lows, like his fall into sin with Bathsheba and even plotting the murder of Uriah the Hittite. Not only that, but the trial points David faced weren't primarily a reflection of his living in a fallen world, either. Instead, they were a direct result of his falling into sin and having to live with the negative consequences (like having a son rebel and try to take his life).

As you look at your life story, do you see a "yo-yo" ride of faith and falling like David? Do you see times of great spiritual strength, but also experiences of stinging personal failure? If so, tell your group you'd place yourself in the David category.

The Jonah Pattern: A Prodigal Come Home

The life of Jonah represents a third overall life pattern. He was the type of person who ran from the Lord at one time but then sought to live out a life of faith.

Almost all of us have heard the story of the reluctant prophet Jonah since we were children. Every man since Adam has tried to hide from God at some time or in some way, but for some men, Jonah's story comes close to mirroring their standard way of life.

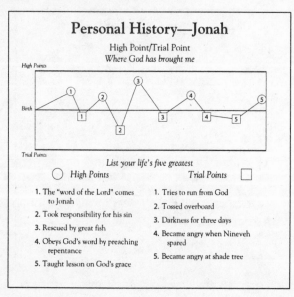

Personal History—Jonah

High Point/Trial Point
Where God has brought me

List your life's five greatest

○ High Points   Trial Points ☐

High Points
1. The "word of the Lord" comes to Jonah
2. Took responsibility for his sin
3. Rescued by great fish
4. Obeys God's word by preaching repentance
5. Taught lesson on God's grace

Trial Points
1. Tries to run from God
2. Tossed overboard
3. Darkness for three days
4. Became angry when Nineveh spared
5. Became angry at shade tree

Jonah tried to run as far as he could from God. Yet he ran into the truth David captured years before in a song:

> Where can I go from your Spirit? Where can I flee from your presence? If I go up to the heavens, you are there; if I make my bed in the depths, you are there. If I rise on the wings of the dawn, if I settle on the far side of the sea, even there your hand will guide me, your right hand will hold me fast. (Ps. 139:7-10)

Perhaps Jonah would have never tried to run from God if he'd taken David's words to heart—but I doubt it. Jonah was dead set on disobeying God and getting as far from Him as possible. Yet in spite of what he wanted, God caught him and brought him back to his senses and Himself.

Perhaps you feel a bit like a Jonah as you enter this group experience. Maybe you've come reluctantly to Jesus, or late in life. In a pilot group I led on this Closing the Gap process, one man had grown up in a Christian home but had not been inside a church for 20 years except to attend an occasional wedding. But when he was "tossed overboard" by a wife who left him, God shook him so much that he came back to Jesus and church—on the first day we started this program!

Maybe you're at a point in your life where you've sunk beneath the waves in your spiritual life, but God has graciously rescued you and given you a renewed or even a newfound faith.

If you feel like a Jonah—that you've been running from God and came back reluctantly—don't despair. You couldn't have come up on shore at a better place. In a small group of committed Christian men, you'll find God's love and acceptance, as well as the encouragement to get up off the beach and get about His work. The men you'll be meeting with know a central biblical truth: *God calls reluctant prophets and wandering prodigals to come home.*

Wandering Prodigals Welcome

We've had you evaluate your life story and, as a Christian, make an overall evaluation about whether it reflects a Joseph, David, or Jonah pattern. Yet we'd be remiss if we didn't mention a fourth group of men who may be in your group—*or may be you.* That's someone who looks at his personal history and can't say with certainty that he has ever truly come to Jesus as his personal Lord and Savior.

If that's your situation, don't set aside this book or walk away from your small group. Instead, sit down with a Christian friend in your group, take out a Bible, and look up Luke 15:11-32. There you'll find the story of the prodigal son, a story that might be better titled "The Forgiving Father."

In Luke's Gospel, you'll see a picture of a son who deliberately snubbed his father and walked out to live his own way. But when his money was gone, so, too, were his friends. He was left empty, starving, and lost in an inhospitable land. But he didn't stay that way.

The Scriptures tell us this man "came to his senses" and decided to get up, turn around, and go back to his father. He woke up one day, looked at the damage done by his sin and selfishness, wanted a way of escape—and found one. The same can be true for you. Even if you've "hit bottom," there's Someone who can lift you out of the darkest hole and take you home.

Perhaps you're starting this "Go the Distance" experience because you're at the lowest point in your life. You couldn't have picked a better place to begin to turn things around. As we've said repeatedly, when a man is broken before the Lord, that's when he's most teachable, most open to "coming to" and "serving" his Father with all his heart. But it takes an act of active repentance, echoing the prodigal's words: "Father, I have sinned against heaven and against you," and the acceptance of God's greatest gift—His Son, Jesus Christ. That's something you can do right now.

This very day, you can stop where you are, bow your head, and humbly ask God for the forgiveness of your sins. You can call on Him to lift you out of the darkness and surround you with His love and light. Through the death of His beloved Son, there's a "way of escape." The Bible puts it this way: "For all have sinned and fall short of the glory of God" (Rom. 3:23). But also, "For God so loved the world that he gave his one and only Son, that whoever believes in him shall not perish but have eternal life" (John 3:16).

If you ask Jesus to forgive you of your sin, to come into your life and be your Lord and Savior, He'll honor that prayer. In fact, in 2 Corinthians 5:17 we read, "If anyone is in Christ, he is a new creation; the old has gone, the new has come!" You can walk in newness of life today by coming to Jesus Christ—and we guarantee you'll have the angels in heaven, not to mention the men in your small group, rejoicing with you. And when you finish your prayer, having sought forgiveness and cleansing, you'll wear the title of "son," not "slave."

You Come to Jesus as a Son, Not a Slave

The prodigal son sought to come back to his father as a "hired servant." But his incredibly loving father would have none of it. We read, "But while he was still a long way off, his father saw him, and felt compassion for him, and ran and embraced him, and kissed him" (NASB).

And while the father then listened to and accepted his son's words of repentance, *he stopped his son from giving the rest of his prepared speech:* "Father, I have sinned against heaven and in your sight; I am no longer worthy to be called your son" (NASB).

That's all he got to say. He never got the chance to ask if he could come home as a slave. His father cut him off and called a servant to do something reserved *only* for sons: "But the father said to his slaves, 'Quickly bring out the best robe and put it on him, and put a ring on his hand and sandals on his feet . . . for this son of mine was dead, and has come to life again; he was lost, and has been found'" (NASB).

A son wears a signet ring; a slave doesn't. A son wears fine sandals; a servant doesn't. Can you see the love of this father as he met his son at his point of repentance and welcomed him back to the family?

There's great joy in heaven and earth when a sinner decides to stop running and comes back home. And I guarantee you, if you've just come to Jesus, there'll be great joy in your small group as well.

But in case you still don't think you're "good enough" because of a troubled past, there's yet another lesson taught in the prodigal son parable that applies to your group—that of the "ungrateful brother."

No Unaccepting "Older Brothers" in a Spirit-filled Group

The story of the prodigal son is really two stories—that of the younger son who ran away and then came home and repented, but also that of the older son who stayed home and wouldn't grant his brother forgiveness. It helps to understand the context of Luke 15 to see what a smashing indictment this parable was of the religious leaders of Jesus' time. Here's how Luke 15 begins as Jesus laid out the three parables of the lost sheep, the lost coin, and the prodigal son:

> Now the tax collectors and "sinners" were all gathering around
> to hear him. But the Pharisees and the teachers of the law

muttered, "This man welcomes sinners and eats with them."
Then Jesus told them th[ese] parable[s].

Do you see whom Jesus told His story to? That's right—a group of "older
brothers." Pharisees and scribes were the only ones not rejoicing at the return
of a repentant prodigal. But that's *not* who you'll find in your group—not if
the members are genuine men of faith. *That's because every man you're meeting with is still very much "in process."*

You may think you have a million more miles to go than those Josephs in
your group, but just wait until you've walked with the Lord as long as they
have. Then you'll see what they know intimately—namely, *they've* still got
a million miles to go in becoming like Jesus!

Growth is a never-ending process this side of heaven. All of us, whether we're
spiritual fathers or babes in Christ, need to close the gap when it comes to
being like Him. Our prayer is that in the course of your time together, every
Joseph, David, Jonah, and repentant prodigal in your group will grow significantly in his faith in Jesus.

Before You Begin the Closing the Gap Process

We've mentioned time and again that the Closing the Gap process is best
accomplished in the context of a small group of supportive friends, and with
your spouse if you're married. Let's look at why that's so before we go any
further.

How would you like to lower the stress level in your life, significantly
increase your resistance to sickness, and actually live longer? No, the answer
isn't a magic vitamin supplement. Rather, it's to be in a small group.

Those are just some of the many benefits that come from being in a small
group, as Gary Smalley and I document in our book *The Hidden Value of a
Man*. Others include greater motivation to face and break negative patterns,
the opportunity to learn new coping and caring skills, and a place to go where
people do more than just know your name—they pray for you by name.

For those men who are married, we strongly urge you to work through and
discuss with your wife your Personal History sheet and the plan you develop
here. In fact, an ideal way to go through this study would be to read through
a chapter yourself, filling out the evaluation tools and exercises at the end
of each chapter. Then describe your evaluation and prayerful projections to
your spouse.

Your wife's role *isn't* to be your policeman or an uncaring "editor." Rather, it's to share her insight as your God-given helpmate and be a loving and honest encourager. Getting her feedback, insight, and encouragement on each aspect of your personal plan isn't abdicating your leadership in the home; it demonstrates it.

For example, in the Song of Solomon (God's blueprint for loving relationships), Solomon's bride gave us a picture of leadership and mutual love as she made this request of her husband: "Draw me after you, and let us run together." In other words, she was asking him to get out front and draw her to him the way God draws us by His love. But she also wanted them to "run together." Like pairs ice skating, you have the man leading and yet the two of them skating side by side. Isolating your spouse from an important process like this isn't leadership, and it certainly doesn't reflect a couple who are "running together."

Even if your wife sees something differently or comes up with a lower evaluation number for you in a specific area, don't become defensive. Remember to give her honor as a joint heir of life. Not only that, but also realize that as your helpmate, she can offer her unique perspective on your life, marriage, fathering, and background. Remember that "fools hate reproof and correction," but wise men welcome it.

What if your wife isn't a Christian? Even if she doesn't know the Lord, sharing your spiritual goals with her can be a positive way for her to see your commitment to Him, and it may be a tool He uses to draw her to Himself!

Go the Distance!

Now that you've filled out and shared your Personal History sheet, it's time to begin work on your Closing the Gap plan of action. You'll read one chapter covering one promise per week for the next seven weeks, filling out the forms at the end of each chapter. Jack Hayford starts us off in the next chapter with a discussion of how he grew in his relationship with God, and how we can as well.

May God grant you many blessings as you seek to go the distance for Him.

A Man and His God

by
Jack Hayford

I'm often asked by men, "Jack, what's the key to your own growth in the Lord?" I'm going to give you the simple answer to that question in this chapter. But before I do, I want to describe a couple of incidents that made painfully clear my need to be highly intentional about developing my relationship with God—the very things we pledge in Promise Keepers' promise 1.

Early in my years as a Christian leader (more than three decades ago), I weathered two faith-shaking "seasons of the soul" that deeply affected my relationship with the Lord. Let me tell you about them, for I've found that discussing these episodes transparently not only encourages men, but it also builds them up in their own faith. Perhaps they'll do the same for you.

Over the years, like any man, I've stumbled along the way and had to deal with things that might have compromised God's call to be His disciple. But none of my stumbles were more potentially devastating than these two incidents. The first saw me nearly fall into adultery. Then, a few years later, the second involved similar feelings. This time, though I maintained full integrity of thought and relationship, the resurgence of my former feelings brought such shame that I came to feel utterly worthless.

I've told this story over the years from a consuming desire that no one else

be entrapped by the same deceit that disarmed me. The lessons I've learned,
in part through those struggles with temptation, have helped me to continue
honoring Jesus Christ and to find victory as a man walking with His God.

It Wasn't Runaway Lust

The first episode developed not from a deliberate, lust-motivated pursuit
of evil. Rather, a spirit of deception confused my mind about a young woman
at my workplace. She was an equally committed Christian, but we allowed a
growing friendship to turn into misguided affection.

My increasing infatuation was not the consequence of any dissatisfaction with my marriage to Anna. Throughout the sordid struggle, I felt the
same love for her that I had on the day we married. Nonetheless, I was grad-
ually being blindsided by an attack of the devil—a "flaming arrow of the evil
one" (Eph. 6:16). The deception progressed through stages: (1) benign friendship; (2) casual attraction; (3) lighthearted banter, with increasing mutual
eye contact; (4) a growing need to compliment; (5) a "wondering" about
"God's intention for our relationship"; (6) a movement toward intimate (but
nonsexual) conversation; and finally (7) a full-blown emotional attachment.

Neither the woman involved nor I had any intention of seducing one
another. But the increasing strength of our human frailty was most certainly
drawing us down a path that would inevitably have led to immorality. Even
though I blindly continued to cooperate with my potential for sin by ignoring the signs of overfamiliarity, I still felt a gnawing fear. It drove me to
frequent times of desperately crying out to God for help, confessing my sin
and asking Him to sanctify my thoughts. But somehow, the chains of my
emotional entrapment had become so rooted that I seemed too paralyzed
to break free.

The worst expression of this deception was a thought that I later came
to see was a classic effort of Satan to persuade me that there was something
"right" about this relationship. Sometimes his most brazen lies present themselves as logical, perfectly acceptable options. As incredible as it seems now,
and as wholly evil as the proposal was, I actually had begun to wonder if God
willed this relationship because of some noble "future purpose" I was to have
with this woman.

At that point in my confusion, however, I was spared further movement
toward an ultimate act of adultery. By God's great grace and mercy, my
despairing cries to Him finally found an answer. It wasn't because of any

strength or discipline on my part—spiritually, mentally, or emotionally. But in a moment of supernatural clarity in my thinking, and by a mighty deliverance of the Holy Spirit, the spiritual entrapment that was rotting my mind was broken. Marvelously, freedom arrived through a powerful encounter with the Lord Jesus! Truly, "Everyone who calls on the name of the Lord will be saved" (Rom. 10:13).

Freed—and committed to stand firm and not let myself be burdened by a yoke of slavery (see Gal. 5:1)—I faced up to the horrifying fact of where that relationship was headed. I immediately took steps to terminate it and disallow any more verbal nourishing of the infatuation. I offered no explanations, no apologies, and set my face to follow a path that Jesus' deliverance opened to me. First Corinthians 10:13 became alive: "God is faithful; he will not let you be tempted beyond what you can bear. But when you are tempted, he will also provide a way out so that you can stand up under it." I set about nurturing my marriage and my relationship with the Lord to renewed health.

Undoubtedly, the delusion that had gripped me would have eventually ruined everything of true value in my life. And God not only delivered me, but He also helped me see a full healing of the emotional pain inflicted on my precious wife. She was wonderfully understanding, patient, and loving, though time was still needed to reestablish comfort and trustworthiness. We moved ahead, refusing to bring up the past, and only after a decade (and then with her permission) did I begin to teach the lessons learned through that horrible time.

Would Lightning Strike Twice?
The second situation was different yet much the same. Let me explain.

More than four years after the first experience, while I was teaching at a Christian college, it seemed that "from out of nowhere" I was struck with confusing feelings of affection for a young woman student. I can honestly say I had done nothing to foster those feelings, and she was completely unaware of their existence. I had shielded my heart with full faithfulness, having learned from my earlier struggle, but nonetheless I again found myself locked in an internal wrestling match. I was stricken with fear, asking myself, *Am I on the brink of failing in spite of myself? Is lightning about to strike twice?*

The "sameness" of this struggle was that it related to inner feelings that I thought were unworthy. The "different" feature was that at no time did I let this girl know how I felt. Still, though I was righteous in my behavior and steadfast in prayer and God's Word, an inner torment—a gnawing fear that said "You're the same old you, and you're going to fail!"—began to beleaguer my soul. The only reason the fear took hold was that it was rooted in my past. But because it was, I labored under something so akin to the heaviness of soul that had consumed me before that the spirit of condemnation became unbearable.

God's grace and providence, however, once again rescued me. This struggle that had brought me to the bottom of depression—not with a deceiving infatuation but with an infernal condemnation—was suddenly broken! During prayer one morning, the Holy Spirit profoundly and powerfully breathed into my spirit from the book of James: "Blessed is the man who perseveres under trial, because when he has stood the test, he will receive the crown of life that God has promised to those who love him" (James 1:12).

That one verse set my soul soaring! As a rocket blastoff lifts a space vehicle beyond earth's atmosphere, so the Word of God set me free. I suddenly saw the *promise:* "He will receive the crown of life." My heart leapt with joy as I thought, *There's a reward for going through all this! I'm not just going through a struggle for struggle's sake!* It was as if the angels themselves were shouting, "Jack, you *have* won! You're going to receive a reward!" And thus the Lord revealed that I was being tested on my earlier commitment to keep my heart pure and my mind clean. Recognizing that my resolve had been challenged and proved steadfast brought me an immediate sense of joy that shattered my depression.

The Bible says, "Do not grieve, for the joy of the LORD is your strength" (Nehem. 8:10). It was true! Joy filled me with strength, and this "follow-up" turbulence of my soul ended with the discovery that I had won a warrior's crown. Anchored by the unshakable assurance that for the rest of my life all resistance to trial and temptation would find victory upon victory as I stood my ground, I passed on to a new phase of my walk with Jesus.

The Enemy's Quest to Destroy Hope

I've described these mental and spiritual struggles for one reason: I want to unmask and bring into focus the predatory evil that assails men on the brink of spiritual breakthrough. Mercilessly and hatefully, the devil seeks every means to destroy hope. I've seen this among men who have been blessed at Promise Keepers conferences. They return home, stirred with a new vision for righteous living and positive change. Yet within days, they crash headlong into a brick wall of adversity; within weeks, their shining hope has become pitted, pock-marked, and stained. "A roaring lion looking for someone to devour," Peter wrote, describing Satan's strategy for defeating us (1 Pet. 5:8). *His goal: to make a man lose his grip on the hope that things can really change, just as that hope is being birthed!* Hope says that tomorrow is going to be worth it, that things can be turned around. Hope causes a man to say, "I *can* become a godly man." That's what the enemy attacks.

Revelation 12:12 describes what we need to know about this spiritual strafing campaign: "He [Satan] is filled with fury, because he knows that his time is short." Our adversary knows his time is limited. He sees more than the *future* coming of Christ as bringing his end; he sees the *present* entry of Jesus into our lives as the end of his capacity to succeed with us. And he knows that the most vulnerable time to attack is at the threshold of our God-given dream of victory in Jesus. He'll tell us we're fake, saying we're unworthy and that the life we're hoping for will never come to pass. And if he can get us to accept his lie, he hopes to break us with the despair and sense of futility that follow. But God has re-created us in Christ for victory (see 2 Cor. 5:17). The key is to "look unto Jesus" and see the pathway to triumph that He models for us (see Heb. 12:1-2).

The Jesus Paradigm in Battle

Jesus is our example for waging spiritual warfare. See what happened when He—filled with the Spirit at His baptism—was immediately driven by the Spirit into the desert to be tempted (see Matt. 4:1-11). His experience teaches us a fundamental principle: *God isn't afraid to send us into the lion's den after we've had a true encounter with Him!*

He knows that only in the fire of our circumstances can purification take place. He also knows that just as His Word and His Spirit enabled His Son to pass the test, so they'll bring us through with our faith and hope intact, because He has made *us* His sons, too (see John 1:12; Heb. 2:10). Tests of faith—the spiritual struggles we face—are not designed to disqualify us from a confident relationship with God, but to purify us for deeper relationship with Him and greater service for Him.

I've learned that to "go the distance" as a follower of Jesus, I need to implement some practical, nonnegotiable principles. And you and I are the same, brother. We need to learn and use truths that empower us—that usher us into such a love relationship with Jesus and His righteousness that no plan of the enemy can distract us. Galatians 6:7-9 presses a point and grants a certainty.

Read closely: "Don't be deceived . . . what a man sows is exactly what he will reap. What is sown to the flesh reaps decay, but what is sown to the Spirit of God reaps a lasting harvest. So don't grow weary when the harvest is slow in coming. If you don't give up, you'll gain its joy!" (JWH paraphrase).

God has inscribed a promise in those verses that speaks directly to our times of struggle. The text teaches two things. First, there are times *after* we've decided to follow Jesus when the harvest of our past keeps coming in. Though we're new in Him, some of the things sown in our past still bear their fruit. Second, however, if we keep sowing to the Spirit—that is, keep pursuing Jesus' way through trial with His power and presence—the time is near when *that* harvest will overtake the old and we'll find ourselves gathering a much better kind of fruit.

Spending Time with Jesus

As I said at the beginning of this chapter, I'm often asked, "Jack, what's the key to your own growth in the Lord?" The answer is so unimpressive and without the sound of intellect or guru-type "wisdom" that I think many men don't really notice how I respond. But this is the answer: *I walk with Jesus every day.*

Usually when I say that, men will follow up by asking for quantities: "How many minutes or hours do you pray? How many days do you fast, chapters do you read, and hours do you study?" But without minimizing the fact that time and diligence are, indeed, a part of our call to discipleship, the bottom line is simply being with Him. Let me offer some guidelines.

First, Start Your Days with a "Sonrise Declaration."

The past couple of years, I've shared what follows with tens of thousands of men in the packed stadiums of Promise Keepers events. I haven't given it a name before now, but let me call this "rise and shine" statement a "Sonrise Declaration." It's the way I *start* my daily walk with Jesus.

When the bedside alarm goes off, I roll my legs off the mattress and kneel. My first act of the day is to bow before my King. I've formed the habit that in those few seconds that follow, I make a faith-grounded commitment to God—of myself and the new day He's given me.

Let me offer this habit for your adoption, not as a legalistic regimen or a kind of "good luck charm" for nice days, but for what it is: a solid-in-the-Word, rooted-in-living-faith, healthy entry into the day. I don't propose it as a substitute for prayer or the discipline of daily devotions, and certainly not a replacement for regular, daily reading of the Word of God. But I've found that it sets my pace as I make a clear statement of my commitment to the One who has made so great a commitment to me. It's not exactly the same every day, and you can adjust it as you wish, but here's a kind of "grid of truth" composed of solid stuff for launching any day—this year or any year:

> Father, I kneel at Your throne to begin this new day. I lift my hands to declare before Your watching angels and any of hell's dark powers: I am a servant of the Most High God! His Son Jesus Christ is my Savior and the Lord of my life! I invite You, Holy Spirit: Fill me afresh for this new day. Make my life a praise to the Savior, and make me effective in all I do, for His glory, as I set out to walk with Jesus through this day. Amen.

Launched with God, every day is a day of promise. His mercies are new every morning, and His great faithfulness is guaranteed to us with every day's dawn (see Lam. 3:22-25).

Second, Don't Let Distractions Discourage You.

It's right and wise to set aside time to "be with Jesus" each day. He seemed to model the morning as best for this, and my experience is the same. But two things tend to discourage men I've met, so let me head off those blockages to blessing. (1) Don't feel a day is lost if you haven't spent a long time in devotions. (2) Don't feel you're hopelessly unspiritual if your mind wanders when you pray.

I pray daily, but I don't feel bound to a rigid pattern of performance. There's no biblical requirement to "punch the clock" with God. But I've learned I need, at least two or three times a week, to "just be" with the Lord, to "wait" on Him (see Ps. 27:14). It isn't necessary to use a lot of words or chatter religious noises to inform Him of my presence; I just enjoy *His*. And if my mind wanders, I pull it back from its meandering but don't feel guilty about it. The Lord Jesus is there—and He welcomes my setting aside time to be with Him.

It was during such a time one day, while trying to deal with wandering thoughts, that I wrote a poem called "Thou, God, Seest Me." Many have told me they've found it helpful. The last stanza reads:

> Then a voice speaks to me: "Child of dust, I know you,
> And it's you I've invited to be
> With Me each day, at that time when you pray,

Whether dancing or weary, you see.
I have never required certain moods of you,
And so never require them of Me.
But I'll meet you there
However you are—
We will dance at times
When your spirit climbs—
Or 'mid wandering thoughts,
I'll forsake you not—
And when words are bare
I'll still hear your prayer.
But keep coming, My child.
Good morning."

Learn to rest in this confidence, brother: God welcomes you and me into His presence without our depending on a pattern of performance to please Him. No ritual, however noble or faithfully executed, earns us a higher approval from God. *We may learn from acquired disciplines, but we never earn through them.*

Please understand that I'm not arguing for sloth or neglect in discipleship. But I've discovered that trying to follow spiritual disciplines and failing to be faithful in them—which is the common human experience—often becomes the most nagging, harassing thing in a man's life. Guilt and self-condemnation breed in the soul, fester, and create a negative mindset that is totally counterproductive to and preemptive of spiritual growth. It's ironic how a sense of duty toward Christian discipline can beget a sense of futility instead. So resist that.

Just learn to "be" with the Lord. Accumulated words or spiritual actions aren't the key to "going the distance" with God; having a heart for Him is. So learn with me the greatest wisdom we can ever lay hold of as believers in Jesus: *The heart of a child inherits the Kingdom* (see Matt. 18:3). Childlikeness of soul, transparency in His presence, and humility before His throne—these are the qualities that bring true growth in our relationship with Him and joyfulness in our service. Looking back over years of experience, I've concluded that the most important thing I can do in my walk with God is to preserve the soft-heartedness of that little boy named Jack who received Jesus when he was 10, keep the teachable spirit of a man who never presumes he "knows" anything completely, and ceaselessly commit to *walk with Jesus every day*.

Third, Read the Word of God—Daily.

Of course, there's no steady development and no practical, eternal guidance for daily living unless you and I get into the Word of God. We advance in direct proportion to our submission to God's counsel: "In all your ways acknowledge him, and he will make your paths straight. . . . Your word is a lamp to my feet and a light for my path" (Prov. 3:6; Ps. 119:105). Let me tell you how I've learned to develop and maintain a solid pattern of daily reading of the Word.

I've always been a regular reader of the Bible, having been raised in a believing home. But *daily* reading seemed to elude me no matter how diligently I tried. I remember launching many a New Year's with chart in hand and setting forth on the traditional "three chapters a day and five on Sunday" regimen. It's true that plan will cover the whole Bible in a year, and it's a goal I've reached a number of times. But it wasn't that way at the beginning.

Somehow I'd "miss" some days—schedule changes, oversleeping, and circumstances all conspired to frustrate my quest for a perfect record. Then came that autumn retreat, nearly 30 years ago now.

I was speaking to some students from a Christian college, and I had just concluded my first evening's message with a call to make specific points of commitment to the Lord. As the musicians played quietly, a prayerful spirit filled the mountain conference hall, and I bowed over the pulpit—simply waiting while the campers prayed. Then the Holy Spirit spoke to my heart: "What are *you* going to commit?"

It's humorous to remember now, but I was completely disarmed by the question. Then, embarrassed, I acknowledged how presumptuous it was that I was "in neutral" while others were geared to pray. It was as though, as the speaker, I had unconsciously succumbed to an attitude of thinking myself only an observer—not a respondent. But now, suddenly alerted by the prompting of the Spirit, I began to pray, asking what the Lord might want to work in me. What happened—as simple as it was—changed my immediate future. And with decades behind me since that date, I can also say that I believe my whole life is different because of what followed that moment.

Thinking on my desire to be a consistent Bible reader, I caught a picture—an idea that distilled into these words: "Don't turn out the light until you've turned on the Light!" Those words became my commitment: "I won't, Lord. With Your help, I will never turn out the light, as I go to bed, without being certain that the Light of Your Word has fed my soul that day." And it worked.

I've become conditioned to associate the practice of turning my bedside light out with the question, "Has the Light been turned on yet today?" If it hasn't, I remedy the problem at once.

Some practical keys to profitable Bible reading:

1. Never read less than a full chapter, daily. Better still, read at least two or three, which takes about 10-15 minutes when done thoughtfully.

2. Never skip around. Read through complete books of the Bible. Place a mark in the table of contents to keep track of your completion of a book.

3. Don't let yourself bog down in difficult passages, such as Exodus' detailed description of the tabernacle's specifications. Break up tough-to-read passages and intersperse with Psalms or Proverbs, for example.

4. Keep a notebook handy, and jot down thoughts the Holy Spirit brings to your mind as you read. But don't get sidetracked into this as a substitute for progress in your reading.

5. Distinguish between "reading" and "study." The former concentrates on coverage, with a look for practical truth as you go. The latter seeks in-depth insights and background and is a separate exercise for classwork or personal enrichment.

6. Never let even the finest study resource become a substitute for your reading of the Bible. Excellent aids can divert your attention, because they do offer good, practical material. They're "helps" and should be used—but the focus in Bible reading obviously needs to be kept on the Bible, not other books.

7. When you're tired, read aloud to help you keep your focus. Always read with an eye to letting the Word "read you"; that is, read with an open heart that invites the Holy Spirit to show you what you need—not what others need.

Let the reality of these verses grip your soul:

"How can a young man keep his way pure? By living according to your word" (Ps. 119:9).

"Like newborn babies, crave pure spiritual milk, so that by it you may grow up in your salvation" (1 Pet. 2:2).

"Do not merely listen to the word, and so deceive yourselves. Do what it says" (James 1:22).

"All Scripture is God-breathed and is useful for teaching,

rebuking, correcting and training in righteousness, so that the man of God may be thoroughly equipped for every good work" (2 Tim. 3:16-17).

The things of the flesh and the world begin to lose their energy in the environment of a Word-fed soul. Read it!

Finally, Bow at the Throne.

Along with the breath of prayer and the food of the Word, we all need the exercise of worship. Of course, worship happens week to week as a man applies the counsel of Hebrews 10:25: "Let us not give up meeting together, as some are in the habit of doing, but let us encourage one another—and all the more as you see the Day approaching." But I've also learned the power of private worship, and I'm convinced that it's both essential and deeply desirable. There's nothing I prod men toward more pointedly than to become *expressive* in their worship.

David was a man's man and a warrior's warrior. The Bible calls him "a man after God's heart," and he stands tall as a man who blessed a nation and served with faithfulness. Even in his failure, he modeled the most insightful and humble pathway of repentance and recovery. Central to all this was one overarching fact: David was a man of worship! His expressiveness—upraised hands, dancing with joy, shouting and clapping praise, lifting his voice to magnify God's mightiness, standing, bowing, prostrate in humility—all flows together to indicate he saw a linkage between his *posture* and his *praise*. His worship as revealed in his psalms points to a man who was "into" worship, and his expressiveness cannot be consigned to a cultural practice—it's presented as a *biblical* one.

I urge men—even if only in private times with God—to "offer your bodies as living sacrifices . . . of worship" (Rom. 12:1). It has a way of moving us out of misty, ethereal notions about God and into a place before His throne where we put our bodies into action—a pledge of the life we intend to live when we leave our private devotions and step into the world of our witness.

Go for It!

Yes, my brother—go the distance! There is nothing beyond belief or reach regarding your potential in Christ. Walking daily with Him is sure to bring you two things: fruitfulness and fulfillment.

They're yours in Jesus!

Closing the Gap
by John Trent

You've just read Dr. Hayford's chapter on promise 1: "A Man and His God." Here at the end of this chapter, and following each of the other promise chapters, you'll find specific tools that can help you create and share your personal plan of action and live as a promise keeper.

First, there are three forms to complete. They're titled "Personal Evaluation Point," "Setting a Prayerful Horizon," and "Action Plan Worksheet." You need to fill out all three *before* your group meeting. Together they form a "baseline" measure of where you are today, as well as the backbone for where you'd prayerfully like to be tomorrow. Then you'll find a list of discussion questions that can be used in your group meeting time.

To demonstrate how each form works, please read through the following hypothetical example. By looking at the life of a man named "Brian" and reviewing his completed forms, you'll see how you're to fill out your own profile forms in this and the following chapters.

Filling Out His "Personal Evaluation Point"

Like you, Brian finished Jack Hayford's chapter on "A Man and His God." After a careful reading, he saw that prayer, reading the Bible, "being" with God in unstructured moments, and worshiping Him were all important elements of a close walk with Almighty God. He then asked himself four important questions in determining his personal evaluation point.

> 1. Have I demonstrated *consistency* in living out what I know to be God's best in this promise area?
> 2. Have I been *committed to growth* in this area?
> 3. Have I been *open to correction* when I haven't measured up in this area?
> 4. *Do important others* see the same consistency and commitment I do?

In short, he looked at how consistently he was now living out this first promise to honor God above all else—not how well he did *last* year or where he *should* be, but where he is today. Then he asked himself how actively he'd sought to learn and grow in this area and if he'd been defensive or willing to accept counsel or correction as needed.

Answering those questions as honestly and objectively as he could, Brian gave himself a preliminary evaluation point of six in this first promise area. He felt he had worked hard at being a committed Christian, yet his prayer life and depth of knowledge of God's Word presented a gap he wanted to close. Then, as a reality check and reflection point, he asked someone important to him—his wife—to give him a mark as well. She gave him an eight because of his consistency in attending church and urging her and the kids to be there as well, and because of the way he had regularly done personal devotions since his weekend at a Promise Keepers conference.

Based on his own reflection and that feedback from someone who knew him well, Brian revised his first personal evaluation point and settled on a seven (see below).

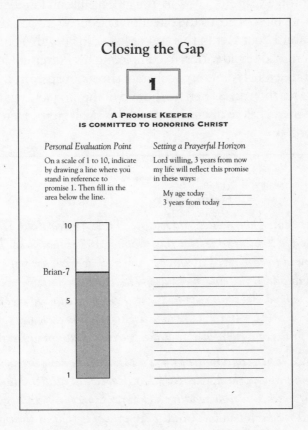

Closing the Gap

1

A Promise Keeper is committed to honoring Christ

Personal Evaluation Point

On a scale of 1 to 10, indicate by drawing a line where you stand in reference to promise 1. Then fill in the area below the line.

Setting a Prayerful Horizon

Lord willing, 3 years from now my life will reflect this promise in these ways:

My age today _____
3 years from today _____

Brian-7

Completing His Prayerful Horizon Form

Brian then moved to write out and picture a prayerful horizon. The goal of this form is to have you look beyond where you are today to where you could be by God's grace and significant effort at a specific point in the future (for our purposes in this book, *three years from now*). Aristotle once said, "A man stands a far greater chance of hitting the target if he can see it." A prayerful horizon is such a target for spiritual growth.

This form provides a picture that isn't bound by questions of "why" or "what if." It's written independent of obstacles like "I don't have any spare time," "I've started and given up on a dozen goals in the past," or "I've never been to Bible school." It's simply a prayerful opportunity for you to say, "Lord, You know where I am today. I want to live for You. Here's what I'd like my life to reflect three years from now as You give me life and strength. I'm open to counsel and, most of all, to the direction of Your Word and Spirit. Please direct me toward Your best in this area as I seek to be with You."

As Brian turned his attention to completing his Prayerful Horizon form, he penciled in a rough draft on a separate sheet of paper. In journal form, he organized his thoughts. Then he showed his horizon form to his wife and even a close friend before discussing it with his small group. Here's his initial prayerful horizon:

Promise One

Setting a Prayerful Horizon

Three years from now, Lord willing, I'll be 43 years old. There are several ways I'd like to reflect this promise and be more like Jesus. I know I need to be more of a man of prayer. I do pray for my wife and children at odd times and most days. But at my horizon point three years from now, I'd like to be praying with my wife at night on our knees before we go to bed. And I'd like to be asking my kids each day something I could pray for them about, and then purposefully pray for them.

I'd also be more of a man of God's Word. I've done pretty well here in reading through the Bible with that devotional guide. However, I sometimes feel I'm just reading a chapter to meet my daily goal, not because I need His daily Word. My prayer is that at the three-year horizon point, I'd have gone deeper in both knowing how to study God's

Word and in digging deeper into the riches there. For me, that means getting and using a study Bible that can help me understand certain passages, and a Bible dictionary to look up key words that I really don't understand.

Finally, I'd be more of a man of worship, particularly when things go wrong in my life. Right now, I tend to go it on my own or just ask for God to "bail me out" when a problem hits. I don't think to praise Him or ask what He's trying to teach me through what's happened. Three years from now, I'd want to be the kind of man who doesn't just "react" when something negative happens. Instead of reacting in anger or jumping to my solution, I want to be someone who slows down and asks the Lord, "What are You teaching me through this event or situation?" and "How can I praise You in spite of, or because of, it?"

As you'll notice, this sheet is an overall, general, prayerful reflection of who Brian would like to become in his relationship with God. It describes certain attitudes he'd like to see and general actions that would mark him as someone who had "closed the gap" on being more like Jesus Christ.

Notice, too, that it took Brian more than one pass to get a prayerful horizon on paper. Also, what he wrote didn't have to be typed out or grammatically correct. It didn't have to be four pages long or worthy of publication. But it should reflect his heart and where he wanted to go after prayerful thought. Then, from this sheet, Brian began to draw out his initial *specifics* that made up his plan of action.

Compiling His Action Plan Worksheet

It takes action—moving forward step by step—for a man to pick out a point on the horizon and reach it. To chart his course, Brian now completed his first Action Plan Worksheet.

Let's look at Brian's sheet, and then at how he went about filling out the three parts found there.

Closing the Gap

1

Action Plan Worksheet

Knowing that I need to improve in this commitment,
I will do my best to take a step of growth by following
through in the three areas listed below:

1. Action Point   *Pray daily, pray at night with my wife, keep a prayer journal to see how God answers my prayer requests.*

Potential Barrier   *Giving up before I give God a chance to answer prayer requests - not keeping the journal handy and accessible.*

2. Action Point   *Read the Bible three times a week, once a week study a passage using commentaries, references.*

Potential Barrier   *Misprioritizing time at work so I end up taking work home and not being able to relax.*

3. Action Point   *Learn not to react when stressful situations arise, but stop and ask myself, "How would Jesus act?" or "What can I learn?"*

Potential Barrier   *Watching television too much, relaxing to the point where I end up falling asleep in front of the TV until late.*

Accountability Commitment

Who   *Bill, Mark, Rich, and Dave (accountability group), my wife*
When   *Once weekly with my accountability group, and once a month "board meetings" with my wife.*

You'll notice on Brian's Action Plan Worksheet that there are three parts to complete. First, there are three action points drawn from his Prayerful Horizon form. These are specific, positive, even measurable actions or attitudes that he could put into practice daily or at least regularly. For Brian, these included goals in relation to his prayer life, going deeper in God's Word, and reacting in a godly way to trials.

Then, referring back to Gary Oliver's chapter on barriers to change (and reflecting on his own tendencies and life history), Brian listed three potential barriers to living out his action points. He knew these were things he had to talk about, perhaps even study or seek godly counsel about, if he was to move toward God's best. In Brian's case, these included a fear of failure (because of a track record of starting but not finishing things), poor use of time at work (which meant bringing home work at night that gobbled up time he could spend on spiritual things), and late-night television.

This third barrier referred to a bad habit he'd gotten into of "relaxing" in front of the television after the late news. Because he felt he deserved some down time, he'd sit and watch a nightly variety program or movie. Unfortunately, instead of relaxing and going to bed with his wife as he should, he'd stumble into the bedroom long after she'd fallen asleep and wake up tired and grumpy the next morning.

By beginning the day worn out instead of rested, he felt he was handling the inevitable problems of the work day less effectively than he otherwise could. Instead of coming to work feeling centered in his faith and having prayed with his wife or read God's Word the night before, he felt anxious, on edge, and unprepared.

These action points and potential barriers formed Brian's first pass in developing a specific plan. As he met with his small group, he knew these items could change as God impressed upon him a more important step or pointed out a more damaging barrier to confront. But he needed to start somewhere. And these initial steps and roadblocks to avoid were the things he discussed with his spouse and small group and asked them to pray about—and hold him accountable to.

I M P O R T A N T

Please Note: If you've been keeping track, Brian came up with three action points and three potential barriers for just this first promise area. If you're thinking ahead, that means he'll have *21* action points and *21* potential barriers that will make up his plan before he's done. Even if there's some duplication of points or barriers (and duplication is fine), that could be as many as 40 different things to keep in mind! *But don't be overwhelmed.* Please keep reading and working to develop your plan until chapter 12. There we'll talk about how you can synthesize and simplify these individual parts into a practical, daily plan of action. What's more, you'll see that as you work through each growth cycle in your small group, you'll focus on only one action point and one potential barrier at a time. That's more than manageable as you seek to move toward God's best.

Finally, Brian penciled in the names of the four men in his small group as the ones who would provide the "Accountability Commitment" to live out his plan. Now he was ready to go on to the next chapter and read, evaluate, and form a plan of action for the second promise area.

Closing the Gap

$$\boxed{1}$$

A PROMISE KEEPER
IS COMMITTED TO HONORING CHRIST

Personal Evaluation Point

On a scale of 1 to 10, indicate by drawing a line where you stand in reference to promise 1. Then fill in the area below the line.

Setting a Prayerful Horizon

Lord willing, 3 years from now my life will reflect this promise in these ways:

My age today _____
3 years from today _____

10

5 - - - - -

1

_____
_____
_____
_____
_____
_____
_____
_____
_____
_____
_____
_____
_____
_____
_____
_____
_____

Closing the Gap

1

Action Plan Worksheet

Knowing that I need to improve in this commitment,
I will do my best to take a step of growth by following
through in the three areas listed below:

1. *Action Point*

_____

_____

Potential Barrier

_____

_____

2. *Action Point*

_____

_____

Potential Barrier

_____

_____

3. *Action Point*

_____

_____

Potential Barrier

_____

_____

Accountability Commitment

Who _____

When _____

That's a picture of how to fill out the three evaluation and planning sheets that follow each chapter. *It's your turn now.* What you come up with doesn't have to be profound, and it isn't something you're doing to "prove" something to anyone in your group. It's just a basic plan of action for a man who's in process, as we all are, but who wants to "close the gap" and "go the distance" for His Lord.

Group Discussion Questions

1. Jack Hayford is candid about the temptations he faced that would have ruined his marriage and ministry. Has there been a time in your life when you've been tempted to toss over your integrity? Tell your group what rescued you and helped you stand firm in the midst of that trial. If you've fallen over the edge of temptation in a major area, how have you dealt with that sin? Have you sought forgiveness, and do you feel forgiven and ready to move on today?

2. Pastor Hayford said, "If I'd been spending quality time with my Lord early in my ministry, chances are I wouldn't have strayed so close to the edge of personal disaster." Reflecting on those words, how would you define "quality time" with the Lord? Is that definition reflected in your action points? Have you seen a direct relationship in your life between facing temptations and spending time "with Him"?

3. Pastor Hayford says that "quality" time with the Lord doesn't always mean "structured" time. What are some creative or unstructured ways you've spent time with God? What successes or challenges have you had in trying to keep a specific daily time with the Lord?

4. Many believers over the years, including Pastor Hayford, have kept a personal journal of their walk of faith. What has been your experience with such journaling? What could you gain now by taking that kind of daily "look back" at your relationship with God?

5. What is your feeling about the encouragement Pastor Hayford gives to worship the Lord with our voice *and* body? Why?

6

A Man and His Mentors

by
Stu Weber

f it hadn't been for Steve McDonald, I don't know if I would have made it. Trauma tumbled in upon trauma. Adversity heaped upon adversity. Obstacle stacked upon obstacle. Test piled upon test. It was way too much for one soldier to handle.

Especially a little soldier.

It wasn't just the tense teachers and emotional moms that got to me. There were lines. Mats. Desks. Rules. Orders. Explanations. Expectations. And girls—more girls than I'd ever seen in one place.

But somehow, on that first terrifying day of kindergarten, Stevie and I found each other and huddled together like a couple of lost puppies. Together, we survived the stressors. We even traded snacks! That may have been the first time I experienced the soul-buttressing impact of what I call "mutual mentoring." But it wasn't the last.

Years later, in 1967, a grizzled old noncom at Fort Benning, Georgia, taught the same principle—in a different way—to a formation of ramrod-straight troops: "Never go into battle alone!"

In what seems like a long time ago in a galaxy far away, this nation was at war in Vietnam. As the war built to its peak, one of the stops for young regu-

lar army officers was the U.S. Army Ranger School at Fort Benning. The
venerable, steely-eyed veteran told us the next nine weeks would test our
mettle as it had never been tested. He said many wouldn't make it—it was
just too tough. (Turned out, he was right. Of 287 in the formation that day,
only 110 finished the nine weeks. And fewer than 90 of those were awarded
the coveted Ranger tab.)

I can still hear that raspy voice cutting through the morning humidity like
a serrated blade. "We are here to save your lives," he preached. "We're going
to see to it that you overcome all your natural fears—especially of height and
water. We're going to show you just how much incredible stress the human
mind and body can endure. And when we're finished with you, you will be
the U.S. Army's best. You will not only survive in combat, you will accomplish your mission!"

Then, before he dismissed the formation, the hardened Ranger sergeant
announced our first assignment. We'd steeled ourselves for something really
tough—like running 10 miles in full battle gear or rappelling down a sheer
cliff. So the noncom's first order took us off guard.

He told us to find a buddy. Some of us would have preferred the cliff.

"This is step one," he growled. "You need to find yourself a Ranger buddy.
You will stick together. You will never leave each other. You will encourage each other, and, as necessary, you will carry each other."

It was the army's way of saying, "Difficult assignments require a friend.
Together is better. You need someone to help you accomplish the tough
course ahead."

It rings true, doesn't it? Think through some of the tough spots in your life.
What difference have friends made in those tight corners and dark valleys?
What difference *might* they have made?

Stevie McDonald became my "Ranger buddy" that first day of kindergarten. We stuck together all year. And we grew. We could hardly wait for
the next challenge. First grade was going to be a piece of cake!

I would never forget that basic life lesson. I'm still practicing it, and the
longer I live, the more I see its validity confirmed. Life is a lot like kindergarten—much easier with a friend.

What Stevie and I discovered in kindergarten, and what the U.S. Army
insisted upon in Ranger school, were just the childhood and military versions
of Promise Keepers' promise 2: A Promise Keeper is committed to pursuing

vital relationships with a few other men, understanding that he needs brothers to help him keep his promises. But long before my discovery in kindergarten, long before that Ranger school formation, and long before the seven promises, the Bible made God's intention absolutely clear: Men weren't made to walk alone. We need a buddy, a fellow soldier, a mentor to walk beside us in the swift-flowing challenges of life.

Jesus Himself reinforced this truth when He sent His guys on one of their early missions: "After this the Lord appointed seventy-two others and sent them two by two ahead of him to every town and place where he was about to go. He told them . . . 'Do not take a purse or bag or sandals'" (Luke 10:1-2,4).

It was Jesus' way of saying, "Never go into battle alone. You don't need a lot of money or equipment, but you do need your friend." He knew that spiritual survival in this world is tough—akin to "lambs among wolves," He'd said. And He didn't want His men trying to go it alone. He didn't want any lone rangers in His kingdom.

Think through the life of another dominant figure in the New Testament. What do these names mean to you: John Mark. Titus. Stephanas. Timothy. Fortunatus. Silas. Epaphroditus. Luke. Barnabas. Epaphras. See any connection? A first-century World Cup soccer team, maybe? The front row of oarsmen in a slave galley? As a matter of fact, they were a team of sorts. And they were certainly slaves of one Master. But what else did they have in common?

Each had a vital relationship with a scrappy missionary-warrior named Paul.

Even a man of the apostle Paul's enormous stature refused to walk alone! In fact, at one point in his career, he actually walked away from an extraordinary open door of ministry because he missed his buddy. "Now when I went to Troas to preach the gospel of Christ and found that the Lord had opened a door for me, I still had no peace of mind, because I did not find my brother Titus there. So I said good-by to them and went on to Macedonia" (2 Cor. 2:12-13).

This singular giant of the New Testament truly was a giant—but seldom singular. He was always with a friend. The list of his buddies never seems to quit. And his darkest moments of ministry came when a Roman dungeon separated him from his fellow gospel soldiers.

When you think about it, it's the same with the most dominant figure in all the Bible. Even God Himself never goes anywhere without His two "best friends"! The Trinity always does it together.

Your need is no different. Whoever you are, you're no stronger than the apostle Paul! You need a few mutually mentoring friends, too. Every pilot needs his wingman. Every soldier needs his Ranger buddy. Every man needs his friends. Do you have yours?

The Power Behind Our Promises

The need for mentoring friendships is particularly keen when it comes to keeping some of life's most demanding promises. I know that if I didn't have some of the close friends around me that I do, I would long since have ended up on some kind of casualty list. And I have a strong hunch you and I are a lot alike.

Like your Lord, your word is your bond. When you break your word, you lose a little of yourself. Because He made you in His image, He expects you— like Him—to be a promise maker and keeper. In fact, He designed promise keeping to occupy a place at the very heart of life. The whole world hangs upon it. It's His mark—like fingerprints—on His creation. God's promises are woven into the warp and woof of the universe. "[The Lord] remembers his covenant forever, the word he commanded, for a thousand generations" (Ps. 105:8).

Think of it. Because God is a promise keeper, this world is not destroyed. Because He's a promise keeper, Israel is still a nation, our sins are forgiven, and our hope is in heaven!

Promise keeping is life. Whether it's taking your son fishing, mowing the lawn, paying a light bill, or standing fast beside the wife of your youth—it all hangs on the thread of a promise. And it all reflects His glory. You can't own a home, buy a car, take a wife, or be a man if you can't keep a promise.

A real man brings certainty into an uncertain world by the power of his promise. Nothing is more important. It just stands to reason, then, that promise keeping is an area of life where we can use all the help we can get. If you could use a friend to help you fine-tune that old Chevy engine in the garage, how much more the engine of your soul?

Treacherous Currents

Whereas God keeps His promises for thousands of generations, today it seems that many Christian men are unable to keep their promises for even one generation. You know the statistics as well as I do. You've seen the devastation just as I have.

I'm thinking of several men right now—and the memories make me wince. These are Christian men in our community that I've known at a distance for years, and they represent many men in our confused culture. One recently decided his wife of two decades was losing her youthful figure. He dropped her for a younger woman. He simply turned his back and walked away from the promise of a lifetime. Another wandered thoughtlessly into his high school reunion and fell into a "summertime infatuation" with an old flame. A third decided he was "happier" with one of his female co-workers than with his wife, the mother of his children.

Those guys were looking for their manhood in all the wrong places. And they lost it. Oh, I know there are "two sides." I know there was some "history." I know there had been some relational pain. I know all that stuff, but to tell the truth, it doesn't move me a bit. Those men betrayed their promises. In so doing, they spit on their very souls.

No, I don't know everything that was happening in their lives. But I can tell you straight up what wasn't happening. Those guys didn't have spiritual Ranger buddies to help them keep their feet under them in the riptides of stress and temptation. They were "loners," men without true friends.

And now they are truly empty men.

Their homes are destroyed. Their daughters don't smile anymore. Their sons are angry young men. And their families will suffer for generations. Little 11-year-old Carey cries at the drop of a hat. Fifteen-year-old Megan runs with the wrong crowd. And unless I miss my guess, 17-year-old Melissa will be pregnant before the year's out. She's looking for love in all the wrong places— just like her dad.

Each of those kids was betrayed by a dad who didn't keep his promises. Each of those dads is a man who failed to "pursue vital relationships with a few other men, understanding that he needs brothers to help him keep his promises." And that promise breaking is killing them and those they love.

"Kids are resilient," you say? Maybe. They're resilient in the same sense a dying rabbit clings to life while clamped in the jaws of a predator. Hear this, please: Kids never fully recover from the broken promises of divorce. Never. The "resilience" is more like resignation, one step short of death. And death is no fun at all.

Hanging On by Hanging Together

In February 1995, four U.S. Army Rangers died in the cold waters of the Yellow River in the swamps of the Florida panhandle. As I read their harrowing story, my mind went back to another February day in that same Yellow River, on that same exercise. Only this was nearly 30 years ago, and I was one of the Rangers.

With the temperature hovering at 27 degrees, my Ranger buddy, Lou Francis, and I stood on the riverbank, watching the angry, swollen current. We knew what we had to do. There was no choice. But that didn't make it any easier! Stripping out of our only dry clothes, we wrapped them and our weapons in our ponchos to form a makeshift floating balloon. Then we eased ourselves into the freezing stream.

Though we considered ourselves better-than-average swimmers, we were quickly overwhelmed by the current. Swept downstream, helplessly gulping more water than air, we both thought we were about to lose our lives—if not to drowning, then to hypothermia. It was sheer terror. But by hanging on to each other, we called up every last bit of energy left in our exhausted bones. Like a couple of drowned rats, we finally crawled up on the opposite bank.

We'd done it! We'd stayed alive! The two of us. In that overwhelming current, we'd really needed each other. Both of us knew we would not have survived alone. Ours was a vital relationship.

Friends can save your life. Literally. Whether it's swimming an unfriendly river, leaning into a hostile culture, or fighting a mid-life crisis, friends can keep you alive.

There are some powerful currents out there. Some treacherous riptides and undertows. Some cold, cruel realities. Life is hard. Marriage can be a challenge. Work can exact a terrible strain on mind and body. Providing for a family can be a constant struggle. Fathering can take its toll. It's not even easy just being a man these days. The margin between "making it" and "not making it" can be razor-thin.

That's where strong friends come in.

Just when you need a little reserve, a little iron in your spine, a little steel in your soul, a little extra oomph to clear the bar, strong friends can make the difference. They can empower you to keep your promises. In so doing, they not only save your life, your career, and your marriage, but even whole families. Even generations. Like the current of a great river, our cultural trends will hurl a man miles downstream—or suck him under—unless he has a friend to help him ride the river.

Pursue Is a Verb

How do you find such a friend, a Ranger buddy? Take a look at promise 2 again.

The main verb is *pursue*.

You get the idea. Chase. Seek. Find. Go after.

You go for it. You get after it. You swallow hard and pick up the phone. You stretch out your hand. You take an interest in someone. You kick aside that natural reserve and open your heart a little. You choke back that lying pride and admit a couple of needs in your life. And you stay at it until you get it done. Eventually, you'll find a man who wants a friendship like that as much as you do.

When that Ranger noncom at Fort Benning dismissed our formation to allow us to find our Ranger buddy, there were some awkward moments. Believe me, most of us men would rather jump out of an airplane than have to practice a little vulnerability. We'd rather crawl on our bellies with live ammo zinging over our heads than have to look someone eyeball to eyeball and suggest a friendship.

In Ranger school, however, we didn't have any choice. That tough little sergeant made us do it. So we did. But no one's giving us orders now—or are they? When you stop to think about it, our Lord Jesus has a lot more authority than that noncom. And He says you need a friend. It's not really optional.

Let's translate some of this stuff into everyday life. When you need—really need—something in your life that you know to be good for you, what do you do? Where do you start? How about on your knees?

Pray

It's a radical concept, but why not give prayer a shot? "Lord, I know I need a friend. You've even told me I need one. But if I'm ever going to find this spiritual Ranger buddy, I'm going to need Your help."

He who knows how to give good gifts loves to do so.

Make a List

Scratch some specifics on a piece of paper, and then put some feet to them. Draw up a list of potential mentoring candidates. You might not even get the names right. You might have to write, "The bald guy who drives the blue

Dodge Ram," "The fellow in church with the squirmy kids," or "The man at the men's breakfast with the Chicago Bulls cap." If you can't even get that far on your list, it may be because you're staying away from church too much. There's an answer for that! Get active. Check into the men's ministry at your church. Ours provides a "clearing house" for men looking for vital relationships.

Bring the names of a few guys before the Lord, and ask for His help. Pray about your approach. Sometimes the easiest first step is to ask several men to form a group with you.

Take the Initiative

Next, your pursuit shifts into passing gear. You know yourself, and you know what it would take for you to really get rolling. For my part, I think a direct approach works best. One technique might be to hand your potential friend this book. Ask him to read this chapter. Tell him you're interested in forming the kind of relationship it describes. If he's willing, schedule a time to get together and talk it through.

Just do it! Refuse to be discouraged if the first few attempts misfire. You've lost nothing—and you've got everything to gain.

Develop Regular Contact

Agree deliberately on your meeting schedule. A face-to-face time once a week is key. Decide when and how. On top of the regular meetings, shake loose now and then and call each other spontaneously with no agenda. It's amazing how encouraging such a call can be! Refuse to be intimidated by setbacks or letdowns. Pursue, pursue, pursue.

Practice Relational Skills

In my book *Locking Arms*, I explain a simple structure called the "4 A's":

Acceptance says take each other exactly where you're at. That's the way Jesus accepts you. This is the *acquaintance* level.

Affirmation means encouraging one another by accentuating each other's positive attributes. We men need and crave respect. And a man cannot affirm himself. Do it for each other. This is the *friendship* level.

Accountability grows over time. As your relationship and confidence in one another develop, and as your acceptance and affirmation take root, you earn the right to ask the "hard questions." Free of anything resembling an accusatory spirit, you probe a little deeper below the surface—to areas where your friend may really be struggling. Strengthen one another as David and Jonathan did. "And Jonathan had David reaffirm his oath out of love for him, because he loved him as he loved himself" (1 Sam. 20:17). This is the *brother* level.

Authority speaks of mutual submission to the standards and values of God's Word. We become, in effect, "God with skin on" for each other, submitting our lives to one another in Jesus. Sound tough? It *is* tough—but well worth it. It may save your promises, your family, your faith, and your very life. This is the *mission* level.

A Little Perspective

Let's backtrack a bit for some perspective. Who was your first friend? Can you name him? Did you have a pal in kindergarten? How about middle school?

Remember the first time you had to put on pads for football practice in the seventh grade? "What goes where?" Danny Wilson and I coached each other every step of the way through that potentially humiliating experience.

Can you recall that first day of college thousands of miles from home? If Bob Davis and I hadn't latched on to one another in that confusion, I think we'd still be standing in some mile-long, serpentine registration line. Talk about bewildering! But Bob was there, with that wide grin of his, and somehow we made it through. (I talked to Bob on the phone just last week. Though we now live a continent apart, that friendship forged under the stress of freshman fear still undergirds my life.)

How, specifically, can friends empower your promises? Let me show you.

Twin Tower Promises

I've made a number of promises in my life so far. But two of them tower over the rest: marriage and ministry.

On a sun-splashed summer day in the fruitful Yakima Valley of central Washington, dressed in my finest, I told Linda Lininger I would be with her all my life. Twenty-nine summers later (some hotter than others), we're still together. There's been a lot of water under our marital bridge, some of it deep; some of it white; all of it requiring careful navigation. But the fact is, we're still riding that river and that promise together. It's a lot smoother and more enjoyable these days. And the best part of the river is still ahead.

Lindy and I are both firstborns. We're both assertive in personality and competitive in nature. She was raised by an extremely abusive father who eventually abandoned the family. I was unsettled in my relationship with my mom in my earliest years. Lindy and I maintain that if *we* can have a meaningful marriage, anyone can.

Some mutual mentors have helped make that possible. I don't know where we would be if those strong Christian friends hadn't come along at strategic moments. One time, a few years back, we actually spent several days away in a cabin with friends, working through the issues of our marriage. We're stronger for it—and how we love those friends!

Let's talk about that second towering promise: the promise of ministry. Not long after our marriage, I was in Vietnam. No tuxedos this time—only military fatigues, mud, and fear that crept in like fog over San Francisco Bay. Yet it was there, more than 25 years ago, at the age of 25, that I committed my life to ministry. It was in the spring, on a hillside in the battle-worn Dak Poko Valley of the Central Highlands. With my face pushed into the bank of a trench and the air rank with the smell of cordite, I began that second promise-making process that resulted in Lindy and me heading for a life in ministry.

Faced with the likelihood of not living out the day—or perhaps even the hour—I began to wonder what "living" was all about. I remember thinking, *Now that I've lived 25 years, how might my life count if the Lord gave me another 25?*

A few weeks later, while on R and R in Hawaii, I held my lady in my arms again and raced on the beach with our little firstborn son. Somehow, it all came into focus in those few golden days of love and laughter. What matters most in life? My family and God's family. My bride and kids and His Bride and kids—the church of Jesus Christ.

So we devoted ourselves to 25 years of concentration on those two families. It was a promise that, like the first one, has governed every day of our lives since. And again, some key friends have helped empower that promise. Without them, I'd hate to think where I might be. And to this day, every time ministry threatens to overwhelm life, one of my yoke fellows speaks courage to my heart.

I've spoken of two towering promises. But while you're with me here, I'm going to make still another pledge. Call it a renewal of commitments. A recent milestone year of my life brought with it both my fiftieth birthday and the completion of our "25-year vow" in ministry. Lindy and I are empty-nested now, and the church family we founded together years ago is healthy and continues to grow. We're at an altogether new season in our lives. And it's about time to renew some promises to govern this new phase.

We're taking another brief R and R and asking ourselves this question: If the Lord should give us another 25 years to live, what's it going to take for us to finish well? We're carefully evaluating how we might best use our gifts and energies to make a difference for Jesus and His kingdom in this season of our lives. We're going to renew our promises to marriage and to ministry. We have no desire to drift; we want our lives to be guided powerfully on the tracks of promise. And if ever we needed friends to keep us pointed in the right direction, it's now.

Three promises. Three seasons. But there's a common thread in each of them. Friends. Lifelong, promise-empowering friends. Brothers who stood with me then. Brothers who stand with me now. They were there in the bewilderment and joy of my wedding day. They were there through the grinding days of seminary. They were there in the faith-testing days of church planting. They've been there in the spirit-enlarging years of marriage and through the heart-rending, soul-stretching days of ongoing ministry.

Let me tell you about a few of those friends and the nature of our relationships.

Vital Relationships Must Center On Vital Issues

The vital mentoring friendships underlined by promise 2 must center on vital issues. We're not talking about weather and sports here. We're talking about the real stuff—the real issues of life. Yes, small talk is a necessary part of every relationship. (You have to start somewhere.) But it's only the preliminary to the main event. The championship rounds must go all the way to the core.

Take a look at that key word, *vital*. It comes from a root meaning "to live." We see it pop up in terms like "vital organs" and "vitamins." *Vital* means necessary or essential to life itself. Without it, you assume room temperature. And in the same way, mentoring relationships must penetrate to the level of life's essence—matters of soul and spirit, of thoughts and emotions.

The first meaningful accountability group I participated in started the same way my relationship with my army Ranger buddy did—by assignment. Years ago, those of us on the staff at church watched in amazement (and some real fear) as pastors all around us were "picked off" by the evil one. Men—even colleagues we had respected—seemed to be failing morally on all sides. We'd heard of the need for accountability groups, so we decided to try it.

About a dozen of us put our names in a hat and drew our accountability partners. I was hoping for a couple of really familiar names—guys who were already close friends. It didn't happen. I couldn't believe the names I'd picked! Of all the men on staff, I couldn't think of two guys with whom I had less in common (or so I thought).

One of our business types? And one of our staff counselors? How could this ever work? Everyone knows administrators are detail guys and counselors are sensitive types. I don't like details and couldn't counsel my way out of a wet paper bag. I groaned inwardly (behind a polite smile) and thought I was going to be one very unhappy camper.

And I was, for a while. We all were. But as that old cowboy song says, "Life is a dance, and you learn as you go." And man, did I learn some things! Our first weekly meetings were bad news. We showed up, said the expected things, and prayed the predictable prayers. Yet each of us frowned inside over the waste of time and the shallowness of the discussion. Each of us wondered when this accountability thing would blow over—and how we'd ever been caught up in some ivory-tower fad like this.

As I look back on those meetings now, I have to chuckle. We didn't have a clue. But we kept slugging away at it, too stubborn to quit.

Then one afternoon, everything changed. The frustration melted away in a single meeting, a single moment. It all began with one of us who decided to take a risk, to step up to the plate.

That one soul opened up—slowly at first, deliberately. But then the dike broke and it all came rushing out. We were stunned for a moment, rocked back in our folding chairs, and then deeply moved. A brother was struggling in his marriage. Deeply frustrated and disillusioned, he'd been drifting. He'd had some wild thoughts and nursed them a bit. He was so disappointed with himself and so ashamed. He was also angry with himself, his family, God—with everyone.

But he was also honest. Real. Authentic. And broken in the group.

Do you think his revelation might have turned the other two away? Do you think they felt like coming down on him? Not a chance! Both wanted to shout out loud, "You too?" Suddenly, it all snapped into focus. We knew why we were meeting. We knew what we were about. All three men saw themselves in the one. And the willingness of the one to risk changed all three.

We began to personalize Scripture for one another. We realized that the secrets each man carried in his chest really were "common to man"—just as the Bible had said all along. Lights went on for us as we found the things plaguing one of our souls were plaguing all our souls.

What a revelation! Those were the magic moments. Our souls bonded. And we couldn't stop. We came to know one another. We had a place to go now—a safe place to bare our hearts. And care. And carry each other. We'd become Ranger buddies, and we were never again going to try to swim those treacherous currents alone.

Our meetings picked up fast and actually became the highlight of our week. No more awkwardness. No more phony clichés. No more going through the motions. We tended to run over the allotted time every week as we talked, prayed, laughed, and sometimes teared up. Shallow moments grew further and further apart.

When we ran out of spontaneous soul sharing, we would begin a more deliberate "Complete this sentence" exercise. And the healthy floodgates would open again. We'd ask one question or make one statement to which each of us would respond—things like "The last time I felt really angry was when . . .," "The last time I really felt hurt was when . . .," or "The last time I felt proud/anxious/ashamed/fulfilled/content was when . . ." We had a never-ending list of masculine emotions and issues to work through together: stress; debt; husbanding; fathering; childhood backgrounds; personality types; eccentricities; hobbies.

We became such good friends that we began doing things together outside of work and ministry. And through it all we learned to carry each other through the turbulent currents that sought to overwhelm us. As adults, we were learning all over again the great lesson of kindergarten, of war, and of the kingdom of Christ: Never go into battle alone!

In time, we did a "fruit basket upset" with those staff accountability groups and mixed the names into new groups. That way, the entire staff could enjoy one another and experience the variety of men God had called together. Then, with the passing of more time, we allowed the men to gravitate toward their natural relationships on the staff. Most of those relationships continue to this day—with life-enriching intensity.

It's an incredible joy for me to see the men relating soul to soul on issues that will matter for a lifetime. And yes, that same detail-oriented administrator is still one of my best friends. I can and do still take heart in hand and run into his office for mutual soul checking. And our new "sensitive type" staff counselor who replaced the original third musketeer knows the ins and outs of my heart and remains a regular confidant. We're determined to help each other (to adapt another of the army's phrases) "be all we can be." And that same joy is spreading through the church now as more and more men find each other in meaningful mentoring friendships through our men's ministry.

Please don't misunderstand. This ain't heaven yet. None of us is running for sainthood. And it hasn't all been smooth sailing. We encounter the same "man common" problems all groups do. We get discouraged over lack of progress. We bog down in scheduling hassles. We stumble over inconsistency. And sometimes the stretches between meetings go too long. Still, the empowering nature of mentoring retains its strength. Just when we're about to wander off into the shallows of superficiality, someone takes another risk, and we're reminded again of how deeply we really need one another.

Mountains in Our Midst

Running the length of the state of Oregon, like a giant spinal column, are the mountains of the majestic Cascade Range. The snow-crowned peak nearest my home is Mount Hood, towering more than 11,000 feet high. Less than 50 miles from my front door, it dominates the horizon. Stately. Symmetrical. Majestic. Serene.

Only trouble is, you can't always see it.

Seasonal clouds and storms rolling in off the Pacific can obscure visibility for weeks at a time. I look out my window, and it's as though the mountain isn't there. It's hard to believe that such a huge hunk of vertical real estate could hide like that. But deep down, below that overcast malaise that settles over us through the long, wet winters, we know it's still there—still knife-sharp, thrusting into the sky; still beautiful; still dominating the landscape and looming over the foothills. There's security in that.

Mutually mentoring friendships are much the same. They're not always visible, but they're always there—solid, stable, and dominating the landscape of our lives. We may not always be conscious of them, but they act like that mountain range spine, putting backbone in our promises. There's security in that, too.

Let me tell you about one of the mountains in my life. John and I have never been part of a formal accountability group together, but our relationship is the most mutually strengthening masculine friendship I've ever had. And it has dominated the landscape of my life for 25 years.

John's friendship has been my "ace in the hole." We've locked arms through thick and thin. We've stomped through the brush and hiked the ridges together as hunting partners season after season. We've worked hard together in the things that matter most. He knows my marriage. I know his. We've raised our kids together. We've taken long drives together, talking. And although we've never had a formally scheduled time together, there are understandings about our relationship that have become almost instinctive.

Like that big, old mountain just out of sight in the clouds, we provide a stable anchor point on the horizon of one another's lives. We call each other regularly. (Believe it or not, he just called, spontaneously, smack dab in the middle of this paragraph, to see how I was doing!) We grab lunch together whenever we can. And our every conversation enjoys the incredible confidence and freedom of knowing "We're safe here." We also know we'd each "go to the wall" for the other.

Let's face it, I need an ace in the hole. I wouldn't be the person I am without John. I wouldn't have the marriage and family I have without him. I wouldn't have the ministry I have. My life is a testimony to the character we've shared together—his life, too. And it gets better with the years. It's a good thing to experience aging together, man to man. I cherish that, and you will as well.

But like anything else worth keeping, you've got to pursue it. Its value is increased by its scarcity. So go for it. Get determined. Get expressive. Get active. And pursue vital relationships with a few other men. It'll make crossing the river so much better.

A Warrior's Farewell
One soldier who'd crossed a lot of rivers with his Ranger buddy said it best. Though his buddy had been killed right beside him in Vietnam, the memories of that friendship continued to warm him and walk with him through

the years. Decades after the war, the old vet left the following note beneath his friend's name on the Vietnam Veterans' Memorial wall. It reminded me of the kinds of things David wrote of his friend Jonathan, who died on the slopes of Mount Gilboa.

"Dear John—The things I'm going to say in this letter are about 20 years and a whole lifetime too late, but maybe that won't matter once they've been said. We trusted each other implicitly. We depended on each other. We supported each other. We shared a whole lot in the time we knew each other: pain, hunger, sickness, triumph, laughter, and more than a little excitement. . . . I never thanked you for the times that you saved my life. Any more than you thanked me for the times I saved yours. I kind of thought that was understood, and didn't matter. It does seem to mean something to me now. It's important. Thanks. . . . I've always said that when you died, it was like . . . the other half of myself. . . . I never got to say good-bye. So I've come to this monument to have a little memorial service and to say good-bye and to let you go. I'll never forget you, don't worry about that. I'm a living testimony that you were good at what we did together."

How about you? Is it adding up for you? Are you giving yourself to a mentoring relationship? Are you opening up to a man friend or two? Do any of your fellow soldiers know where the chinks in your armor might be? Are you locking arms with a soul mate, a Ranger buddy? Some dark day when your knees are weak, the current is swift, and the water is cold, you'll be glad you did.

Closing the Gap
by John Trent

You've finished reading the chapter "A Man and His Mentors," by Stu Weber, which speaks about promise 2. Now it's time to complete the forms that follow. These are the Personal Evaluation form, where you give yourself an overall 1 to 10 rating on living out this promise; the Horizon Point form, where you sketch out a written picture of the man you would like to be three years from today; and three action points and potential barriers to fully living for Jesus in this area.

If you have questions about these forms, see the end of chapter 5, "A Man and His God."

Closing the Gap

$$\boxed{2}$$

A PROMISE KEEPER IS COMMITTED TO PURSUING VITAL RELATIONSHIPS WITH OTHER MEN

Personal Evaluation Point

On a scale of 1 to 10, indicate by drawing a line where you stand in reference to promise 2. Then fill in the area below the line.

Setting a Prayerful Horizon

Lord willing, 3 years from now my life will reflect this promise in these ways:

My age today   _____
3 years from today _____

10

5 - - - - -

1

_____
_____
_____
_____
_____
_____
_____
_____
_____
_____
_____
_____
_____
_____
_____

Closing the Gap

$$\boxed{2}$$

Action Plan Worksheet

Knowing that I need to improve in this commitment,
I will do my best to take a step of growth by following
through in the three areas listed below:

1. *Action Point*

_____

_____

Potential Barrier

_____

2. *Action Point*

_____

_____

Potential Barrier

_____

3. *Action Point*

_____

_____

Potential Barrier

_____

Accountability Commitment

Who _____

When _____

Discussion Questions

1. Describe a time when you couldn't have made it through a situation without the help of a friend, teammate, co-worker, or someone else. What did that experience teach you?

2. Stu Weber points out that God is a promise keeper, so that's what we should be, too. In fact, he says that "promise keeping is life." Do you agree or disagree? Why?

3. Review the five things Stu suggests for finding a "Ranger buddy." Write them in the spaces below, then ask each other these questions:

Which of these will be easy to do? Which will be hard? Why?

a. _____

b. _____

c. _____

d. _____

e. _____

_____

_____

_____

_____

4. What would you do if you approached someone about being a mentor and he turned you down?

5. Stu mentions four things that characterize biblical friendships. They are acceptance, affirmation, accountability, and authority. A relationship starts with the first, then each builds on the one before it. Think about your two closest relationships with men. Do they reflect the pattern seen here? Why or why not? What can you do to insure the relationship moves closer to the things Stu talks about?

6. Another key point of this chapter is that vital relationships must center on vital issues. Kick the following questions around with the guys in your group.

a. Are you willing to be as vulnerable with the guys in your group as the guy in Stu's group? Why or why not?

b. What's your biggest fear in letting the walls down around your life?

c. What do you have to gain by being vulnerable enough to let the other guys know where your weak spots are?

d. If there was a ever a "man's man" in the Bible, it was the apostle Paul. Divide these passages among the group, read them aloud, then discuss what they say about his vulnerability:

Romans 7:18-25
2 Corinthians 1:6-8
2 Corinthians 11:23-30
2 Corinthians 12:9-10
1 Timothy 1:15-16

e. How do you get to the point where you're willing to be vulnerable?

A Man and His Integrity

by
Charles W. Colson

I n 1969, I received one of the most exciting phone calls of my life. President Richard Nixon wanted me to be his special counsel, to leave my successful law practice and move to an office down the hall from his.

It meant a great financial sacrifice: My practice was earning well in the six figures, which was a lot of money back then. But I had known Richard Nixon for many years, admired him greatly, and had bright visions of what could be accomplished in his presidency. At 39, I found the thought of working directly for the president of the United States intoxicating. It took me only a few minutes to make up my mind.

To this day I remember walking into the Oval Office, a room that seemed larger than life, with the Gilbert Stuart painting of Washington hanging over the fireplace, the Great Seal of the United States sculpted into the rug, the room flooded with light. Nixon slowly got up, grinned, grabbed my hand, and said, "Good to have you on board, Chuck." Little did I dream in that triumphant, heady moment what was to come in the next years of the Nixon presidency. If I'd had any idea, I might well have turned and run for my life.

Instead, of course, I did what any self-respecting, young Yankee from Boston ought to do. Not wanting to give even the appearance of a conflict of interest, I took everything I had earned practicing law—nine successful years—and put it in a blind trust in a Boston bank. No one would point an accusing finger at me.

I had grown up in a puritanical home. My dad, who was the son of a Swedish immigrant, had a rigid sense of right and wrong. "Never tell a lie," he used to warn me when I was a tot. "Always do the right thing, keep your conscience clean, work hard, and you'll get ahead." My dad was the Protestant work ethic personified. And surrounded by corruption in Massachusetts politics, I believed passionately in good government. I knew it was high time Americans had the government they truly deserved.

In fact, that Puritan ethic was so well ingrained that I even told my law partners and clients not to visit me during the four years I would be in the White House. I was, as I realize now, thoroughly self-righteous. People would frequently send gifts to me—boxes of candy at Christmas, alcohol, or passes to theaters—and I would invariably give them to my limousine driver or the switchboard operators in the White House. One time someone came to my office and was seeking a government favor. In the course of that conversation, he mentioned how much money his group had given to the Nixon campaign, and I told him to leave my office on the double or be thrown out.

No one was going to corrupt me. I had studied in college about Kant's categorical imperative: "Act as if the maxim of thy act were to become by thy will a universal law of nature." Heady stuff, and I swallowed it hook, line, and maxim. I truly believed that with my intelligence, experience, and will, I could remain above reproach. I imagined that I could promise myself to be an upstanding man—and that would be that. There was no need to bring God or anyone else into it.

I ended up going to jail.

So much for the idea that through my own resources and the rational process, I not only knew what was right but would actually choose to do it. So much for Kant's categorical imperative. So much for the idea that I alone, unguided by God, could live a consistently good life. So much for self-righteousness. In fact, we are never in greater danger than when we're self-righteous.

Can We Be Good Without God?

Jeremiah understood this: There's nothing more deceitful than the human heart (see Jer. 17:9). But that's a hard admission. How much more glorious to believe we can act righteously, with integrity, without God. Yet the result of breaking ranks with God has been devastating, both in personal terms and in a national sense. Many intelligent people fear we'll lose our liberties as the government responds to the resulting increasing moral anarchy. I confess to sharing that fear, for history has shown that if you take away a nation's Bibles, you'd better start polishing the bayonets. This is why what we do as promise keepers is not only important to our families and ourselves, but to our nation as well.

So how do we remain righteous? Can we be good without God? The answer is emphatically no. Can we be men of integrity, people who keep the third of the seven promises of a Promise Keeper? Again, the answer is no.

It's true, of course, that atheists can do decent, noble things. Nominal Christians often are involved in good works. But I submit that when push comes to shove, when people are under great stress, they may know what's right, but they haven't the will to live out a life of integrity.

There's a great moment in Tolstoy's *War and Peace* when Pierre, the central character, shakes his fist at the sky and says, "Why is it I know what is right and do what is wrong?" Tolstoy was writing, as did the apostle Paul in Romans 7, about the ongoing battle with the fallen human will, which can be subdued only by the transforming power of Jesus Christ.

As promise keepers, we've been transformed and can now live with strength, assurance, and joy. We make our promises to God, and God responds with the greatest promise of all—to remain faithful to us. Paul reminded us of this bedrock fact: "For I am persuaded, that neither death, nor life, nor angels, nor principalities, nor powers, nor things present, nor things to come; nor height, nor depth, nor any other creature, shall be able to separate us from the love of God, which is in Christ Jesus our Lord" (Rom. 8:38-39, KJV).

Let me tell you how I came to make my promise to love and obey God, a promise He has responded to by changing my life forever, just as He has transformed the lives of countless millions of Christians who dared to take Him at His word. Then I would like to speak about our duty to God and how this duty, far from being an imposition, is actually an expression of our devotion to Jesus Christ, the glory of our faith, and the key to a life of utter integrity. Never forget: The history of Christianity is a history of promises made and kept. These promises have changed the world and offer the world its only lasting hope.

Inner Changes Impossible to Overlook

My spiritual journey began after I left the White House in 1973. I had everything a person could want, or so I thought. I was a close friend of the president of the United States. I was told by the first Watergate investigators that I was not a target of their inquiry. I went back to my law firm, where I had a half-dozen clients each willing to pay me over $100,000 a year. I had a chauffeured limousine, a yacht in Chesapeake Bay—every material advantage.

And I was miserable. I went through a long period of wondering what life was about, feeling empty and dead inside. At first I wrote it off to having been in high government office under tremendous pressure, beepers on my belt going off at all times of day and night, the president calling me in, being in the midst of crises around the world—it seemed like three or four going on at any one time. That's enough to exhaust anyone, so I waited for the gloom to lift, like a soldier returning home from active duty.

But even after I'd been out of the White House several months, I continued to feel that emptiness inside, something I just couldn't explain. Many of you have been in this same position. Life is good, as the commercial says, yet there's no peace.

In this dark night of my life, I met with an old friend, Tom Phillips. Tom was chairman of the board and CEO of the Raytheon Company, one of the largest corporations in America. Raytheon had been a client before I went to the White House, and I was back in his office once again to be his counsel.

I knew immediately that I was speaking to a changed Tom Phillips. Something was different about him and his office. His desk was clear. He was smiling, relaxed, asking about my family and how I was weathering the political storms. This was not the usual small talk one carries on without thought or feeling. Tom really seemed to care. It was discomfiting.

Minutes into the conversation, I said, "Tom, you've changed. What's happened to you?"

Quick as a flash, he said, "Yes, I've changed. I have accepted Jesus Christ and have committed my life to Him."

I had to take a firm grip on the bottom of my chair. Tom's words were stunning, especially coming from a man of his stature. What could he mean? I had studied Jesus when I'd gone to Sunday school as a kid. I knew Him to be an ancient, historical figure, a good, moral man whose teachings give us the basis for what we know as Christianity. And I considered myself a Christian. After all, I grew up in America, it's a Christian country, I wasn't Jewish, I went to church twice a year, so I must be a Christian. Case closed.

How was I to understand those simple words Tom had just spoken? This man was an engineer, scientist, business executive—and he was talking about Jesus as if He were there right at that moment. I put on my best smile, the one we wear whenever we're called upon to tolerate our friends' eccentricities, and quickly steered the conversation far afield.

But when we met over the next months, the difference in Tom was impossible to overlook. He was at peace—somehow transformed into a serene man who genuinely cared about me. I, on the other hand, was in increasing anguish. I was now in the midst of the Watergate debacle, the biggest American political upheaval in a hundred years. Washington was ugly. I was depressed and mad at myself, though I couldn't admit it. I was dead inside.

In this state, I went to see Tom at his home outside Boston one hot August night—a night that forever changed my life.

"Tell me, Chuck," Tom asked after we had taken our seats on a screened-in porch, "are you doing okay?"

Like a good lawyer, I deflected the question and asked Tom how he was doing.

He quickly reviewed his past—his business and personal triumphs—and then spoke words that could have been spoken by me: "The success came, all right, but something was missing. I felt a terrible emptiness. Sometimes I would get up in the middle of the night and pace the floor of my bedroom or stare out in the darkness for hours at a time."

I told Tom I didn't understand how this could be. "You were a straight arrow," I said. "Good family life, successful—everything, in fact, going your way."

"All that may be true, Chuck," he responded, "but my life wasn't complete. I would go to the office each day and do my job, striving all the time to make the company succeed, but there was a big hole in my life. I began to read the Scriptures, looking for answers. Something made me realize I needed a personal relationship with God. Something forced me to search."

Tom then told me he had given his life to Jesus during a Billy Graham crusade in New York's Madison Square Garden. "I asked Jesus to come into my life, and I could feel His presence with me, His peace within me. I could sense His Spirit there with me."

I was completely puzzled. "That's what you mean by accepting Jesus—you just ask?"

"That's it, as simple as that."

The conversation then turned to Watergate, and I offered a stirring defense of our actions, explaining to Tom that Washington operated on the dog-eat-dog philosophy and that we were only doing what was necessary for the good of the country. Yet the words didn't ring true to me, even as I spoke them.

Tom seemed to sense this. "Chuck," he said in a firm but gentle voice, "I hate to say this, but you guys just brought it on yourselves. If you had put your faith in God, and if your cause were just, He would have guided you. And His help would have been a thousand times more powerful than all your phony ads and shady schemes put together."

Talk about accountability! But Tom wasn't finished. Thank God he wasn't.

Integrity Begins with Honesty and Humility

"Chuck, I don't think you'll understand what I'm saying about God until you're willing to face yourself honestly and squarely," Tom continued. "This is the first step." With that, he picked up a copy of C.S. Lewis's *Mere Christianity* and suggested I take it with me. But just as he was about to hand me the book, he stopped and said he would like to read one chapter.

As he read "The Great Sin," Lewis's devastating critique of human pride, I felt a burning sensation as my face flushed. Tom continued reading, and my discomfort built. Then the words became so truthful, so penetrating, that I was defenseless before them.

"In God you come up against something which is in every respect immeasurably superior to ourselves. Unless you know God as that—and therefore know yourself as nothing in comparison—you do not know God at all. As long as you are proud, you cannot know God. A proud man is always looking down on things and people; and, of course, as long as you are looking down, you cannot see something that is above you."

Suddenly, I felt naked and unclean. The words seemed to sum up what had happened to all of us at the White House: "For pride is a spiritual cancer; it eats up the very possibility of love, or contentment, or even common sense."

Tom knew I was in turmoil, and as I prepared to leave, he asked if I would pray with him. I had never prayed with anyone except to say grace before a meal or recite prayers in church, but it was just Tom and me on his porch, so I said that would be fine. He began, "Lord, we pray for Chuck and his family, that You might open his heart and show him the light and the way."

I cannot describe fully the feelings that came upon me as we prayed. I was driven to the edge of tears and held them back only with supreme effort. After the prayer ended, there was a long silence, after which I said good-bye to my friend.

I made it to the driveway and into my car—and could then hold back no longer. In a flood of tears, I gave myself to Jesus Christ—and so began the greatest chapters of my life, a life no longer lived merely for Chuck Colson but a shared life centered on the promises I've made to God. This, the greatest night of my life, came in August 1973. I've felt that same freedom from the penalty of sin ever since, up to and including today. I've known it in bad times and good, for it's real and abiding.

It's real because Jesus Christ is real. As a matter of fact, as I reflect on the years since that night and think of all the great things that have happened to me—the Templeton Prize, best-selling books that have won awards, speaking to parliaments and government leaders all around the world, a ministry that has spread like wildfire to 75 countries—what I'm most moved by is the realization that the Son of God was crucified on the cross to take upon Himself my sins. He died in my place. Because of Him, I can be free.

That realization creates in me the deepest sense of gratitude. So it should be with all of us. Think about it: The Son of God went to the cross, took our sins upon Himself, and died for us. That's an historical fact proved by overwhelming evidence. I couldn't live with myself were it not for His sacrifice for me.

So how do we respond? By going to church Sunday morning, giving a bit of our income, and doing a good deed once in a while? May it never be! The only proper response to what Jesus did for us is that we lay down our lives for Him. We must recognize that with grace comes responsibility and an old-fashioned, almost quaint concept these days—duty. Without a sense of duty—of keeping our promises to obey and serve God—our faith would be nothing more than a pleasant set of maxims, and we would never become men of true integrity.

Duty and Integrity

Christians have fulfilled their duty to God in countless ways, and as promise keepers, we should make such stories part of our consciousness. I don't mean to sound flip, but these stories are much more important than, say, baseball statistics and song lyrics. They're the stories of our faith in action—proof of the power God has invested in His people. They never fail to inspire me and keep my spirit strong.

These stories start, of course, in Scripture. Recall the wonderful story in Matthew 8 of the centurion who told Jesus his servant had been laid low by the palsy. Jesus offered to go to the centurion's house to heal the man, but the centurion said, "But just say the word, and my servant will be healed. For I myself am a man under authority, with soldiers under me. I tell this one, 'Go,' and he goes; and that one, 'Come,' and he comes. I say to my servant, 'Do this,' and he does it" (vv. 8-9).

Jesus' response: "I have not found anyone in Israel with such great faith." And then, "Go! It will be done just as you believed it would" (vv. 10,13).

And his servant was healed at that very hour. The centurion understood duty—and Jesus described it as the greatest example of faith.

One of the most dramatic modern examples of faith and duty involves a friend, John McCain, now a U.S. senator but in the late 1960s a navy commander imprisoned in North Vietnam. His testimony reminds us of the power of prayer, especially in keeping us true to our Christian duty. "The way we got into prison wasn't because of God," McCain wrote recently. "It was because we were rendering unto Caesar that which was Caesar's, because our countries were at war. It wasn't right to ask God to free me. I thought I should leave that situation only if it were in the best interests of my country.

"In 1968 the Vietnamese offered me the opportunity to go home. I had a broken arm, a knee I couldn't walk on without crutches, and I weighed about 100 pounds. I wanted to go home more than almost anything in the world. But our code of conduct says the sick and injured go home in order of capture, and there were others who had been there longer. I knew they wanted to release me because my father was commander of U.S. forces in the Pacific. It would have given them a propaganda victory. I prayed for the strength to make the right decision. And I'm certain those prayers helped me to do what I had to do. I had to stay there."

Like the centurion, John McCain understood duty. He was a man of integrity.

One of the many beautiful things about our Christian faith and duty is how they transform the most unpleasant situations into triumphs. I met a Czech in 1991 whose life is a great example of this power. In fact, my encounter with him has forever changed my view of Christian service.

His name is Vaclav Maly, a handsome man whose face, framed by curly, black hair, might have been chiseled by Michelangelo. When I was introduced to him, he grinned, and in an instant we embraced. He has a warm, vibrant spirit, exuding Christ's love. One could never tell all he had been through.

Ten years earlier, Vaclav Maly, then a youthful priest, was defrocked by the communists because he adhered to his faith rather than to their demands. He was forced to clean toilets in the Prague subway. As it turned out, this humiliation did nothing to undercut Father Maly's authority. It was, in fact, only one more failure of communism.

Instead of being diminished, Father Maly's popularity grew, for this outrage re-emphasized the difference between the gentle and loving priest and his tormentors. As communism crumbled, huge crowds would call for him to address them during demonstrations. During the Velvet Revolution, nearly a million people shouted out, "Maly! Maly!" and Maly led them through the streets to a great outdoor service. That night, faced down by the huge crowds, the tanks and troops fled. Czechoslovakia was free.

As one formerly involved in the political world, I assure you that any politician would covet the adoration and power Maly enjoyed. The temptation to translate personal popularity into political popularity is one of the greatest temptations facing mankind. Yet when Vaclav Havel, the new president, offered Maly any job he wanted in the democratic government, Maly declined. He was, after all, a priest and had a higher calling. He told the president he only wanted to preach the gospel.

When I told him what a hero he was to many of us in the West, he answered, "Oh, no, I am no hero. A hero is someone who does something he doesn't have to. I was just doing my duty."

Of course. Each of us is simply doing what he has to do. If we think about it, it isn't heroic or remarkable. It's simple obedience growing out of devotion to Jesus, our duty to God.

But not all are famous like McCain or Maly; there are countless everyday Christians doing their duty, often in unpleasant circumstances. Prison Fellowship is a ministry in prisons, an ugly setting where I'm nonetheless constantly reminded that there are many saints among us. I recall one prison where an inmate stood and said, "Ten years ago, I was in this prison, and two of your volunteers came in, Mr. Colson, and befriended me, this couple from Akron, Ohio. They've been visiting me every month and writing to me ever since, for 10 years. I get out of prison in September, and they've invited me to live in their home. I'm going to make it."

I have another friend who regularly goes into the AIDS ward of a prison, where people die in his arms. Why do people do this sort of thing? Out of devotion to the categorical imperative? To serve an illusory god? Simply because it makes them feel good?

No. You may go into the AIDS ward a time or two to make yourself feel good, but you don't go repeatedly, year after year. You may even write letters to prisoners out of a desire to give yourself a sense of personal commitment, but you don't invite an ex-con to come live with you. No, this is the Spirit of God at work. The anonymous soup-kitchen worker, the unheralded Angel Tree coordinator—each gives of himself or herself for the same reason that my great model, William Wilberforce, the British parliamentarian, stood in the House of Commons and denounced the slave trade, then worked for the next 20 years until it was ended.

Duty, of course, is not the most popular notion in these days of rampant individualism. In fact, it wasn't even understood by many from the '60s and '70s generation. Their concept was, "We all do our own thing."

The Christian does his duty—keeps his promises—but he doesn't operate in a vacuum. We need to be accountable to one another, both to stay focused and to be encouraged. Breaking promises can be much easier than making them. Never forget the admonition found in Hebrews: "Let us not give up meeting together, as some are in the habit of doing, but let us encourage one another—and all the more as you see the Day approaching" (10:25).

It's all too common, when faced with a strong challenge to our integrity—on the job, in the home, or elsewhere—to fail the test when we try to do it on our own. But making ourselves accountable to Christian brothers can multiply our strength many times over, providing the difference between keeping our promises or going down to defeat.

Surrounded by Strength

That's why I urge all Christians not only to attend services regularly, but also to establish small groups of other Christians to whom they're accountable. I've seen this simple practice work wonders in my own life. In fact, I would never have developed real Christian maturity merely by staying home, reading religious books, and attending church once a week—no more than an athlete can develop by shooting baskets alone in the driveway. We're all parts of a larger Body, and as parts we can't operate alone. Nor is the Body fully formed when some of its parts are not fully integrated.

After I became a Christian, I was surrounded by some loving brothers: Doug Coe; Harold Hughes, a liberal Democratic senator from Iowa; Graham Purcell, an ex-congressman and judge from Texas; and Al Quie. They made it clear from the beginning that they would meet with me regularly. We agreed that I'd make no decisions without them.

Why is this necessary? Even if Christ lives in you, and even if you're a committed disciple, there will be times when temptation will be nearly overpowering. We know that all too well from the unfortunate falls of Christian ministers. We must also remember that we're self-deluding creatures who are fully capable of rationalizing the worst sins, even as Christians. Remember the story of David and Nathan? David, a man after God's own heart, couldn't see his own considerable sin, and Nathan had to tell him the story of a man's obvious sin. David was enraged and told Nathan the man should be punished. Only then could Nathan say, "You are the man!"

I credit my early spiritual growth to that prayer group. They stayed with me. And let me make this clear: By the act of one of those men, I was convinced beyond a shadow of a doubt that Jesus is who He says He is.

Al Quie was no ordinary man at the time of this incident. He had spent 20 years in Congress and was the sixth-ranking Republican in the House. He was greatly admired around Washington. I was in prison for my part in the Watergate scandal. Believe me: Powerful political figures don't make a habit of showing solidarity with those in prison. Al was different.

I was hurting, to put it mildly. As so often is the case, at a time when it seemed life could hardly get worse, along came another problem: One of my sons was arrested for drug possession. At any time, that would be a crushing blow. In this case, the effect was more pronounced because of my imprisonment. I've never felt worse. My son was in trouble, and I couldn't help him.

Powerful politicians look out for themselves. But not Al Quie. "I've been thinking," Al told me soon after the arrest. "There's an old statute someone told me about. I'm going to ask the president if I can serve the rest of your term for you."

I was so moved that I could barely stammer a protest.

"I mean it, Chuck," he continued. "I haven't come to this decision lightly. Your family needs you, and I can't sleep while you're in prison. I'd be a lot happier being inside myself."

Al wasn't the only one. After our conversation, Doug Coe sent me a letter saying that *all* the brothers in our group were willing to serve out my sentence. From that moment to this, I've known Jesus is real. The sacrificial love of those brothers made this undeniable, even though I declined their offer.

Now, let me be the first to admit that over the years I've been tempted to sin. I've done things wrong without even knowing it, because the human heart is deceitful. So the accountability of a small group is indispensable. We have a rule at Prison Fellowship that I will make no decisions about anything of significance without first checking with the executive committee. And I hold myself fully accountable to them.

Let me give you one illustration. Several years ago, I wanted to move to Virginia from Florida because I thought I needed to be nearer to my office. (Prison Fellowship headquarters are in Virginia.) I went to my accountability group, six men on the executive committee, and unanimously they told me not to move. They said I'd be swallowed up in the office, that I'd get involved in administration, that I should be free to write, think, and be creative. So they vetoed the idea, though I really wanted to do it. But I stuck with my accountability, and in hindsight, I'm convinced they were right. I could give many similar examples.

Even more importantly, this group can tell me when I'm off base. A group has the wonderful ability to get us to focus on God rather than ourselves. We may resist this, but without a group, we will likely never recognize how out of focus we're becoming. The result, I'm sad to say, is that God becomes only a small part of our lives.

What else keeps me mindful of my promises to God, particularly this one to be a man of integrity? A contrite and repentant heart.

A Repentant Heart

Repentance—now there's an idea that's often ridiculed in our day, but let me assure you: A repentant heart is vital to our Christian life and the maintenance of integrity. Not a day goes by that we don't sin, at least in thought. We must remember that when we sin, we've turned our back on God, and we're not restored to right relationship without asking forgiveness. The best policy, the one I try to follow, is to immediately ask forgiveness when we realize our sin. Don't keep a backlog of "sins to ask forgiveness for." Don't delay even until nighttime prayers. Pray without ceasing, and seek forgiveness whenever your sin becomes known to you. Otherwise, that backlog grows and, eventually, is ignored. Repentance keeps our relationship with God fresh every moment of our lives.

Repentance, of course, walks hand in hand with guilt, and we've all heard the modern refrain of how guilt is bad for us. There's something to that, although the secular world addresses the problem by saying there's no sin and, therefore, nothing to feel guilty about. And Christians are said to be simplistic. In any case, the Christian response is different. Christians ought not to be haunted by guilt. Jesus died for our sins. If we're genuinely repentant, we've been forgiven. But I never go to communion, for example, without stopping to think about my failures, my omissions, my shortcomings, my pride—all the things I know are working against the obedient Christian life—and seeking God's forgiveness.

Always remember: Practice makes perfect. When we get out of the habit of repenting, it's hard to get back into it, just as it's hard to get back into the habit of daily Scripture reading and regular meetings with a small group. Marx once said that religion is the opiate of the masses—another of his errors. Quite the contrary is true. It requires a great deal of discipline and, as has been said before, constant acts of duty to remain strong in our faith. Christianity is not a passive undertaking.

I'm also blessed because I have a wife who's not impressed with the trappings of power and celebrity. She tells me the way things are. (I dedicated my first book, *Born Again*, to Patty as the one who gets me up when I'm down and brings me down when I'm up. Everyone needs that balance.) Promise Keepers helps build strong families by bringing the family under the dominion of God. One way to glorify God is for Christian men to remind women of their central place in the family and of the value of their counsel. Pray with your wife, and covenant with each other to help one another maintain spiritual balance and integrity.

Also important is to surround ourselves with that which glorifies God and keeps Him fresh in our minds. We'll be better off if we don't spend so much time watching television but leave plenty of time to read. Besides regular Scripture reading, I've been greatly inspired by many of the Christian classics, including Bunyan's *Pilgrim's Progress* and C.S. Lewis's *Mere Christianity*. Such books not only keep us strong in spirit, but they also motivate us to do our duty. And that brings me to my final point.

Promise Keepers isn't just another self-help group, even as Christianity isn't just another lifestyle choice. Promise keepers, your nation needs you. For in you Jesus dwells, and our nation urgently needs the steadying and redemptive hand of Jesus Christ.

Not to belabor the obvious, but look around. Our culture is collapsing. A third of our nation's children are born in illegitimacy, crime is nearly out of control (and is fully out of control in some areas), and our entertainment industry has made decadence its guiding star. There is, in short, moral chaos all around us. How will this be changed? By government programs? A new series of self-help books? How empty our dreams of reversing our cultural chaos if we don't put God at the center of our lives and act out of obedience to Him!

Let there be no doubt: The promises you make to God and your family, including the promise to be a man of integrity, are not parochial matters. They're of life-and-death importance to this nation.

But we'll never rebuild our culture—we're beyond the point of reversing our decline—unless the people of God get serious. We can't believe we're being Christians by singing our hymns, giving our tithes, and going off and living the rest of the week as pagans. One of the books I read while in prison was Dietrich Bonhoeffer's *The Cost of Discipleship*, in which he made it clear: "When Christ calls, He bids a man to come and die." That says it all. We really aren't our own possession but God's. That's a hard lesson, to be sure. It's also the glory of our faith.

If we dedicate ourselves to dying comfortably in our beds, with a pious prayer on our lips, I believe we're betraying Jesus, ourselves, our families, our heritage, and our country. I say this in full recognition that the fight ahead is no mere schoolyard scrap. The powers we face will test us to our utmost. But God has provided. I have at times been utterly desperate, exhausted, and had nothing to work with—physically, emotionally, or spiritually. And then I've prayed for the Holy Spirit and have felt His presence. I know He's real and that God will sustain us through Him.

In the midst of strife, I'm also reminded that those who make their promises to God are bound to one another. Society can be healed, as promised by God in this wonderful passage from Ephesians 2:

"In Christ Jesus you who once were far away have been brought near through the blood of Christ. For he himself is our peace, who has made the two one and has destroyed the barrier, the dividing wall of hostility, by abolishing in his flesh the law with its commandments and regulations. His purpose was to create in himself one new man out of the two, thus making peace, and in this one body to reconcile both of them to God through the cross, by which he put to death their hostility" (vv. 13-16).

I carry with me, tucked in the back of my Bible, a copy of a brief letter written by John Wesley five days before he died. It beautifully captures the interworking of obedience, duty, faith, and fellowship. It was sent to a young William Wilberforce, a member of Parliament crusading against the slave trade, who must have felt weary and beaten down at times.

We must remember the times in which it was written. Slavery was widespread. Its defenders were politically and economically powerful. One defender warned that Wilberforce's proposal to abolish slavery would affect the trade on which "two-thirds of the commerce of this country depends." That's a compelling argument in the halls of power.

But the criticisms went deeper than that, actually attacking the center of Wilberforce's being. The very thought that someone would object to slavery on religious grounds was ridiculed. We're all too familiar with that criticism. We, like Wilberforce, are constantly told that Christians and other religious people should not let their beliefs "infect" public life.

The same advice was given to Wilberforce. "Humanity is a private feeling, not a public principle to act on," scolded the Earl of Abingdon. Lord Melbourne, sounding much like a member of People for the American Way, sniffed, "Things have come to a pretty pass when religion is allowed to invade public life."

But Wilberforce had made his promise to love and honor God with all his heart, soul, and mind. He would be obedient, a man of steadfast integrity. And so he persevered. But he didn't act in a vacuum. One night, after a defeat in the House of Commons, he reread the letter from Wesley, who had recently died. We can consider that this letter is carbon copied to everyone who professes Jesus Christ.

My Dear Sir:

Unless the Divine power has raised you up to be as Athanasius contra mundum [against the world], I see not how you can go through your glorious enterprise in opposing that execrable villainy, which is the scandal of religion, of England, and of human nature. Unless God has raised you up for this very thing, you will be worn by the opposition of men and devils, but if God be for you who can be against you? Are all of them together stronger than God? Oh, be not weary of well-doing. Go on in the name of God, and in the power of His might, till even American slavery, the vilest that ever saw the sun, shall vanish away before it. That He that has guided you from your youth up may continue to strengthen you in this and all things, is the prayer of,

Your affectionate servant,

John Wesley.

Wesley's promise was true. Wilberforce persisted, and against all odds, slavery was ended. A great revival spread through England as a result.

The promise is true for us as well. He who guided and strengthened Wilberforce and Wesley strengthens all who submit to His love. That is the unshakable promise on which I have staked my life. I have not, for one moment, ever regretted it; and with God's grace, I will stay my course and keep my promise.

Closing the Gap
by John Trent

You've finished reading the chapter "A Man and His Integrity," by Charles Colson, which speaks about promise 3. Now it's time to complete the forms that follow. These are the Personal Evaluation form, where you give yourself an overall 1 to 10 rating on living out this promise; the Horizon Point form, where you sketch out a written picture of the man you would like to be three years from today; and three action points and potential barriers to fully living for Jesus in this area.

If you have questions about these forms, see the end of chapter 5, "A Man and His God."

Closing the Gap

3

**A PROMISE KEEPER
IS COMMITTED TO PRACTICING INTEGRITY**

Personal Evaluation Point

On a scale of 1 to 10, indicate by drawing a line where you stand in reference to promise 3. Then fill in the area below the line.

Setting a Prayerful Horizon

Lord willing, 3 years from now my life will reflect this promise in these ways:

My age today   _____
3 years from today _____

10

5 - - - - - - -

1

_____
_____
_____
_____
_____
_____
_____
_____
_____
_____
_____
_____
_____
_____
_____
_____
_____
_____

Closing the Gap

┌─────────┐
│   3   │
└─────────┘

Action Plan Worksheet

Knowing that I need to improve in this commitment,
I will do my best to take a step of growth by following
through in the three areas listed below:

1. *Action Point*

_____

_____

Potential Barrier

_____

_____

2. *Action Point*

_____

_____

Potential Barrier

_____

_____

3. *Action Point*

_____

_____

Potential Barrier

_____

_____

Accountability Commitment

Who _____

When _____

Discussion Questions

1. Chuck Colson says that when he went to Nixon's White House, he was convinced he had all the equipment he needed to choose right from wrong. Have you ever felt like that? Is that what you think now? Why or why not?

2. Chuck also drills home this point: You are never in more danger than when you're self-righteous. Look at these passages, then talk about the following questions: Proverbs 16:18; Jeremiah 17:9-10; 1 Corinthians 10:12.

   a. How can you tell the difference between confidence and pride?
   b. What are the telltale signs of pride?
   c. Does your life bear any of those signs? If so, what can you do to avoid falling prey to your pride? (See Prov. 11:2 and 1 Cor. 10:13 for help with that answer.)

3. C.S. Lewis wrote, "In God, you come up against someone who is, in every respect, immeasurably superior to yourself. Unless you know that . . . you do not know God at all." What things in your life keep you from fully comprehending this truth? What can you do to make it more of a reality?

4. Chuck talks about the need for a deep sense of gratitude for what Jesus has done for us. How should that show itself in the way we live? Think of it this way. If you were about to die in a burning building and, against all the odds, someone raced in to save you, what would you do for that person to show your gratitude?

5. This chapter also talks about the need for a return to a sense of duty in laying our lives down for Christ. Reread the three stories Chuck tells (about the centurion, Sen. John McCain, and Vaclav Maly). Which one hits the closest to home for you? Why? What does that man's experience teach you about living out our faith with a sense of duty?

6. Chuck told a stirring story of what his small group was willing to do for him (i.e., take his place in prison). On a scale of 1 to 10, 1 being "no commitment" and 10 being "willing to go to jail for each other," where is your group? Mark your response on the chart below, then discuss your answer with the other guys in the group. As you mark your answers, keep this in mind: *Be*

honest. Few groups could honestly say 9 or 10, especially if you've only been together a short while.

1	2	3	4	5	6	7	8	9	10

No commitment   *Willing to go to jail*

    a. What's the general consensus of the group about where the group is at?

    b. What would it take to move you closer to a 10?

    c. What's the biggest risk in moving toward a 10? The biggest payoff?

7. The chapter closes with Chuck observing that the fight ahead is no school-yard scrap, which means we must rely on God's Spirit to sustain us when the going gets tough.

    a. Reread John Wesley's letter to William Wilberforce at the end of the chapter. Imagine that you've been fighting the greatest powers in England over an issue that could ruin the livelihood of some rich and influential folks (which is what Wilberforce was doing). How would you have felt when you read Wesley's letter? (Wesley, by the way, was one of the greatest Christian figures of the last 500 years.)

    b. Read the following passages, and talk about the impact they should have in sustaining your integrity when the going gets tough.

        Psalm 33:13-22
        Psalm 118:8-9
        Psalm 147:10-11
        Isaiah 40:27-31
        Philippians 4:11-13

A Man and His Family

by
Gary Smalley

In the first five years of our marriage, my wife, Norma, and I experienced severe trials, big-time discouragement, and deep dissatisfaction with each other. But since then, we've learned some great truths for staying in love and enjoying a strong, lasting marriage. (We've now been married 31 years at the time of this writing.)

That our marriage has survived and even thrived over the years is a tribute to our Lord. In addition, by His faithfulness and grace, and by instilling these valuable truths in our children, all three of them are also happily married and in ministry with us.

Our marital journey—with all its struggles, defeats, and victories—has taught us what strengthens a marriage and what damages one. What we've learned about navigating the marital waters comes not only from our own observations and experiences, but also from the testimony of hundreds of other couples through seminars, books, counseling, and research. By drawing on this collective wisdom, we hope to help you go the distance in fulfilling promise 4: *A Promise Keeper is committed to building strong marriages and families through love, protection, and biblical values.* (Much of the content of this chapter is adapted from my book *Making Love Last Forever*.)

Lack of Training

Unfortunately, Norma and I started our marriage with little training. In premarital sessions, our pastor asked me whether I loved Norma—right in front of her. How could I say anything but yes? When he asked if I would lay down my life for her, I had no idea what that meant. For all I knew, it meant shoving her out of the way of an oncoming truck or taking a bullet for her. So again, I said yes. But no one ever really explained to me how to love a woman sacrificially day by day or how to communicate meaningfully. I think I was given a book to read, but I had little time for any serious study. We both just figured love was enough.

I didn't know then of my need to understand what makes a marriage work. I didn't have mentors and role models to profit from. Worst of all, I didn't pay attention to Norma's marriage manual (the one built into every wife!). If I had sought out these helps, I could have spared myself, my wife, and our family so much grief.

I wasn't aware, for example, that your family of origin affects all attempts at relationship building. I grew up in a stormy home with a father who was a merchant marine. He was always angry, constantly belittling other members of my family. Ducking verbal blows, I saw my dad and mom engage in countless shouting matches. I cringed as I witnessed my father hit my older brother and knock him across the living room. I watched my father distance himself from his family for days—not speaking a word to Mom or any of us kids.

Once, before I was of legal driving age, I got into big trouble when a friend and I decided to take a drive in the family car. It was a fairly new two-door Ford, my dad's pride and joy. As we were backing it down the driveway, my friend looked to see how close I was to a dirt bank. But instead of rolling down the window to look, he opened the passenger door. It caught on the side of the bank, bent back, and nearly ripped off completely.

My heart instantly froze, fearing my father's wrath. We bent the door back in place as best we could. I knew I was going to die as soon as he found out. The next morning, Dad drove off to work without noticing the damage. But when he came home that night, he screamed and hollered about a hit-and-run driver. By then I had already told my mother, but now I wished I hadn't. She wasn't going to keep my secret from Dad, but she did say she would tell him who had done it only if he promised not to blow up at the guilty person. He agreed, so Mom told him. As soon as the words were out of her mouth, he exploded all over me. Not only was I disciplined severely, but I was also closed out of his life for days.

Unfortunately, I unconsciously picked up Dad's habit of shutting people out and tended to do the same in my relationships. The four years I dated Norma "on and off" were mostly "off" because I would just stop calling her whenever things didn't go exactly the way I wanted. For weeks on end, I kept her in the dark, refusing to see her and freezing her out of my life. Then I'd just as mysteriously snap out of it. Only after we married did she tell me how much hurt I had inflicted on her during those four years of dating.

At the time, I didn't realize that unresolved anger inflicts so much damage on a marriage and family. Current, carry-over, and collateral damage—all ran deep within the soul and extended across the generations! I ended up behaving much like my dad—despite my best (but naïve) attempts to be everything he wasn't.

Because my mom and dad had a very unhappy marriage, that's the kind of marriage I soon found myself in—and wanted out of at times. Without a positive role model in my father, I felt a deep hunger to discover what it takes to enjoy your mate and stay in love. Through continuous prayer and education, I came to learn hundreds of ways to sustain a good, satisfying marriage.

I will only touch upon a few of them in this chapter. But the countless ways of love can all be summed up in one equation we learned from John Gottman, whose research into thousands of marriages concludes: *No matter what methods are used to strengthen the marriage, the husband and wife must wind up averaging five positive deposits into each other's emotional bank accounts for every one negative withdrawal.*

Emotional Bank Balance:
Do the Positives Outweigh the Negatives in
Your Relationship?

Marriage is like an emotional bank account. For the relationship to be happy and fulfilling, at the end of every day, week, month, or year, you must have averaged five positive, energy-producing, enjoyable experiences for every negative experience that strained the marriage and drained its emotional reserves.

The following list of positive deposits and negative withdrawals is developed from Gottman's material and observed or experienced in my own and other marriages. You and your mate can do the accounting to see whether the positives outweigh the negatives in your relationship.

Positive Deposits	Negative Withdrawals
• Praise for contributions and ideas	• Criticize contributions and ideas
• Showing affection	• Withholding affection
• Actively listening	• Showing disdain, scorn
• Being understanding	• Being argumentative, defensive
• Being cooperative, participatory	• Being controlling
• Accepting of differences	• Disapproving of differences
• Fun-loving, joyful, good-humored	• Sullen, gloomy, biting, moody
• Treasuring, showing honor	• Disgracing or shaming
• Edifying, enhancing, enlightening	• Defaming one's character
• Showing interest, eye contact	• Disinterest, indifference
• Responding with encouragement	• Uncaring, unresponsive
• Opening a closed spirit	• Being unforgiving, hateful, angry
• Demonstrating genuine empathy	• Falsely interpreting motives
• Validating ideas and feelings	• Degrading, discounting
• Affirming boundaries	• Bullying, creating an unsafe atmosphere
• Being connected, involved	• Isolated, detached, withdrawn
• Being soft, tender, gentle	• Harsh, heavy-handed, escalation of anger

Let me expand on two of those withdrawals from my own perspective and experience, and then I'll explain the four positives we put into motion more than 25 years ago to ensure that our marriage and family could go the distance.

Two Huge Marital Risk Factors:
Escalation and Withdrawal in the Face of Conflict

Two of my favorite researchers on marriage are Drs. Howard Markman and Scott Stanley of Denver University. (They also studied under Dr. Gottman.) They've discovered the main risk factors that can predict with 90 percent accuracy whether marriages will succeed or fail. As they say in their book *Fighting for Your Marriage*, it doesn't matter how committed you are to your mate or how much in love you are when you enter marriage. Rather, *how you resolve daily conflicts* determines whether you'll stay together in a satisfied relationship or eventually divorce.

That's why one key risk factor and predictor of divorce is the *escalation* of arguments. In other words, whenever there's a disagreement, it tends to escalate into a screaming match, where name-calling and blame replace problem-solving tactics.

The opposite pattern, *withdrawal,* is even more likely to lead to divorce. Withdrawal is when one or both partners respond to conflict by distancing themselves, clamming up, building walls, and becoming cold, unemotional, and detached. Partners who go into this mode usually avoid all touch—in the hallways and in bed. Even eye contact may be nonexistent. Such withdrawal—emotional, spiritual, mental, and physical—can reach great lengths, lasting as long as one mate can hold out or as long as one person wants to punish his or her mate.

Some people will use just one of these patterns when conflict occurs. But many others use both. First they'll blow up, escalating the argument. Then, when they run out of steam, they'll withdraw.

Early in our marriage, I specialized in withdrawing. Norma absolutely hated it, which is partly why I did it. In humility and embarrassment, I must confess that I was trying to punish her. Night after night, I lay on the far side of the bed, not speaking to her. Once, when she reached out to touch me, I pushed her away. My shove knocked her out of bed, against the wall, and onto the floor! After that, she didn't feel much like speaking to me, either, and the memory still grieves me today.

On another occasion, I wanted to camp in the Colorado mountains, taking the whole family in our mobile home for three weeks. But after two miserable weeks, Norma and our daughter, Kari, urged me to take them back to Phoenix. I got so angry that I didn't speak to Norma most of the way home.

As we approached Flagstaff, my son Greg confronted me and said, "Dad, is this the example you want to give Michael, Kari, and me?" He reminded me that "Mom is really hurting, and she needs you. Dad, it also hurts me when you won't talk to any of us." With tears welling up, he whispered, "I love you, and I feel alone when you shut us out."

That confrontation finally made me realize what I had been doing. I confessed my sin and promised Norma I would never again withdraw and close her out of any kind of conflict. Now I'm ashamed of such withdrawal behavior, but before then I didn't understand how much damage I was inflicting. The day after a conflict and withdrawal incident with Norma, like the one in Colorado, we'd hug and kiss, make up, and go on. But I never really cleared the air or sought her forgiveness. We essentially ignored the problem, hoping it would just go away. I didn't know this had far-reaching consequences, leaving us both unfulfilled and dissatisfied in our marriage.

Unresolved Anger: The Major Destroyer of Relationships

Escalation and withdrawal are both the result of anger. So resolving anger is key to staying in love. By examining our own marriage and counseling with others, we've discovered more than 10 extremely negative consequences for a person who hangs on to anger. Like rope tied around our feet or hands, anger restricts and binds us, tying us in internal knots, so that we can't even walk in the light of God's truth but are left to grope in darkness (see 1 John 2:9-11).

Long-lasting, unresolved anger also distances us from our loved ones and deafens us to their point of view. Our anger, like a veil of darkness, blinds us to the love of God and others. When angry, we don't see the havoc we create.

Norma and I have firsthand experience with the destructive effects of anger. She has carried around a lot of hurt, frustration, and fear from all the times I used to offend her. She hardly ever felt safe around me, because she wasn't sure what I would say next, what I would demand from her, or whether I was going to withdraw into myself or escalate an argument.

"Our Ways Are Not God's Ways"

Just the other day, Norma reminded me of some of my self-centered ways during the first 10 years of our marriage. There were the times she'd make a delicious meal, excited about learning to cook, and wait for me to come home from work. But I'd run in, change my clothes for a basketball game (which I'd forgotten to tell her about), and blithely skip the meal. With tears filling her eyes, she'd say, "Honey, I made this meal just for you tonight. I was looking forward to being with you."

Invariably, I'd say crudely, "Hey, just put it in the refrige; I'll eat it later." If I was in a nicer mood, I'd ask her to change her plans and come with me to the game. Still, the special meal together wouldn't materialize.

Back then I didn't consider Norma's feelings or needs much at all, mostly because I was absorbed in my own vocational goals or sporting activities and blinded by my own anger. She said I wasn't being mean to her intentionally; it was just my nature to be self-centered. Then I heard a speaker at church expounding on self-centeredness, and I saw just how insensitive I was.

Finally, I realized that self-centeredness is at the root of anger. Think about this: Anger and frustration are the emotions we feel when reality falls short of our expectations. So when we expect something from somebody or expect something to happen in a certain way and our desires aren't met, it isn't reality that triggers our anger so much as it is our self-centered expectations.

Now I see exactly why my father acted the way he did. He was angry because he had a lot of self-centered expectations that were unfulfilled. I adopted the same attitude. If Norma or the kids didn't do what I wanted or expected of them, I became angry.

Later, I came to see how a man's anger, rooted in self-centeredness, dishonors his wife and family. Norma and I were following a dangerous path.

"Lord, Teach Me to Forgive and Get Rid of This Anger."

I was so humbled when I discovered this truth—10 years into my marriage and family life—that I fell on my knees immediately, confessing my sin of self-centeredness: "Lord, teach me to forgive and get rid of this anger." That was my prayer day and night for several months. I was angry at Norma, but I was even angrier at certain Christian leaders for the way they had treated me years before. My daily resentment toward one leader in particular had a debilitating effect on my spiritual life.

I worked hard on the relational "glue" to bond our family together, but my angry outbursts or sullen withdrawals dissolved that bonding and chilled all feelings of warmth or attachment. Now I know why Paul called dads aside and urged, "Fathers, do not exasperate your children" (Eph. 6:4). Again, in Colossians 3:21, the apostle looked parents in the eye and warned, "Do not embitter your children, or they will become discouraged." Children who grow up embittered and angry are emotionally handcuffed, which prevents them from discovering their potential.

I realize now that being angry or relating to others lovingly is my responsibility. When I choose to be angry and express it in ways that control other people, I must confess that as a sin. Sinful expressions of anger are always counterproductive. "For man's anger does not bring about the righteous life that God desires" (James 1:20). However, not all experiences or expressions of anger are sinful. Anger is caused by being fearful, frustrated, or having our feelings hurt—all very human emotions. Paul told us, "In your anger do not sin" and "Do not let the sun go down while you are still angry." Otherwise, we provide a foothold for Satan to work his destructive mischief (see Eph. 4:26-27). Anger serves us well when it motivates us to do good for the Lord and others. But if left unresolved, it destroys relationships.

These biblical and practical truths scared me out of a stagnant marriage. I learned and practiced how to forgive. This is essential to a loving, lasting relationship. When we seek forgiveness from those we've provoked, we release them from the gripping ropes that cut off life-giving circulation. We're also freed ourselves, untying the knots that hold us captive.

My Greatest Discovery:
"What a Great Deal Christianity Is!"

In Jesus Christ I found freedom in forgiveness *and* the source of true fulfillment. Over a period of months, I learned to look to Him for meaning, joy, and ultimate acceptance. And in the process, I was released from *expecting* my wife, my kids, my friends, or my job to give my life purpose. My wife was not my God or my main source of life, strength, or encouragement. *Jesus* was. Therefore, I was free to honor her by asking what *she* needed. Now God could use me to channel His love to her.

This discovery was the greatest thing that ever happened to me. You can make the same discovery. God will be faithful to the man who seeks to build a strong marriage and family. But you must seek after the Lord with all your heart, placing no other gods before Him. When I did that, Jesus gave me the strength to honor and love my wife.

What a great deal Christianity is! When you love the Lord with all your heart and confess your sin, He freely forgives you. Jesus gives you power through His Spirit to live His commandments, which lead us into a loving and lasting relationship with our wife and family. All that for free! In addition, He gives us eternal life. What more could a person ask for? And His eternal life starts as we receive His Spirit within us.

Norma and I wanted God's wisdom about what it takes to have a meaningful relationship so we could help more people in troubled marriages. So, every day we'd ask, seek, knock . . . and God has faithfully granted our request.

Four Basic Commitments

We incorporated what God taught us into our marriage and now pass it along to you. We made four basic commitments that have deepened our love for each other. And marital experts tell us these are the keys to staying in love for the long haul.

(1) We committed ourselves to a journey of continuous education, learning ways to honor each other and make our love last.

(2) We drafted a marriage constitution that would govern our behavior toward one another in our formative years as a family. The primary article of that constitution deals with honor.

(3) We made a commitment to meaningful communication every day. Along the way, we discovered one method for conflict resolution that has helped many couples avoid the major risk factors that lead to divorce.

(4) We committed ourselves to a healthy small group, one that supports us and holds us accountable for our marriage and family values.

Let me expand on each of these.

1. Continuous Education

Once I woke up to how I was hurting Norma, I had a deep hunger to pursue whatever it takes to enjoy one's mate and make love last forever. Because I hadn't had a good example in my father, I resolved to embark on a lifelong journey of learning. That decision was made during the fifth year of our marriage, when Norma was most discouraged with my patterns of withdrawal and escalation. I, too, was discouraged with our marriage. Our arguments were often left hanging. Positive physical touching was not frequent or fun. This plateau was followed by a sharp decline. We feared that in five to 10 years, we'd be out of love.

I remember sitting at the breakfast table of our first little home in Rockford, Illinois, when I asked her, "Norma, what's wrong with our marriage?" and "What would it take to move our marriage toward a 'perfect 10'?"

That's when we first committed ourselves to a path of continuous education, learning how to keep loving each other and growing in our marriage—whatever it took.

At first I feared not being able to go the distance—that it would take more out of me than I had to give. The more we talked, the more I didn't get it. I asked her to tell me one more time what she thought was at the root of our problem.

From my actions, she said, she felt as if everything else on earth was more important to me than her. She patiently repeated the message until I realized, for the first time in my life, that I was dishonoring her by making her feel less valuable than practically everything (TV, sports, my ministry) and everyone else.

From that day on, I decided to treasure Norma above all those people and things. I made that commitment out of my love for God, who is my first love.

To be honest, that was a terrifying thing to do. I feared that Norma would take advantage of me and that my life was over, at least all the fun parts. How wrong I was—again. Norma did just the opposite. As I began treasuring her, making her "number one," her anxieties relaxed, and she became more calm. She enthusiastically pushed me into things she knew I loved to do.

"What a Privilege It Is to Be Her Husband!"

Honor is at the heart of all loving relationships—with God, our spouse and kids, our boss and co-workers. To honor someone is to attach high value to that person. It's a *decision* we make regardless of our *feelings*. When we decide to honor someone, we're saying the person is extremely valuable and important to us.

Biblically, we express honor by how we talk to and treat someone. For example, "Husbands, in the same way be considerate as you live with your wives, and treat them with respect [honor] as the weaker partner and as heirs with you of the gracious gift of life, so that nothing will hinder your prayers" (1 Pet. 3:7).

A football analogy will illustrate my point. To honor your wife is to treat her as the Most Valuable Player on the team, applauding and appreciating her efforts. Like the star quarterback, she is capable of calling the plays without "coaching" from you. You encourage her and listen to her viewpoint and ideas. To honor your mate, in football terminology, also means protecting her the way an offensive lineman protects the quarterback.

My MVP is Norma, whose *autographed* picture graces my office. I praise God daily for my wife and her growth *and failures*. Specific words of praise, focused on character qualities, are not self-serving but show my appreciation. Praising her is the true, noble, right, pure, lovely, admirable, and excellent thing to do (see Phil. 4:8). I praise her when things are going well *and* when she and I are in one of our down times. What a privilege it is to be her husband! I feel "awe" at the opportunity to live with my MVP wife.

Praise is one biblical distinctive of a godly man. Yet many men don't give compliments of any kind for one reason or another. However, repeated, reinforced compliments work wonders in bringing out the best in others.

If your wife doesn't seem receptive to praise, or if you feel awkward verbalizing compliments right now, *write down* those things you appreciate about her. Focus on the way she does what she does, who she is, and what makes her so special compared to all other women. Look every day for qualities in your wife to praise.

"You Ought to Order Those Tapes"

I went in the opposite direction from praise a few years ago while we were in Hawaii with some of our family and staff members. Norma and I had a romantic hotel room on the sixteenth floor overlooking the bay. One morning, I got up early to have a discussion with her about our marriage goals for the following year. Instead of starting the day with something romantic and encouraging, I wanted a "meeting." She knew meetings would mean potential conflict, so she didn't want to do it right then. I pressed my point above her objections, reminding her that we're in the marriage business full time. "Shouldn't we be living what we teach?" I asked peevishly.

She reacted by saying something that equally offended me. Our argument escalated into a full-blown, hour-long discussion—but not about our marriage goals. Then she went to breakfast, leaving me alone in the room, burning with unresolved anger.

Soon knocking on the door was our son Greg, a doctoral student in marriage and family counseling. Having seen his mother so upset, he asked me what I had done. How embarrassing! "I dunno," I fumbled. "It happened so quickly."

A few moments later, Norma's best friend came into the room and said, "Nice going. Now you've wrecked my day, too. She's not speaking to me, either."

Norma and I both worked on the situation all day, finally warming up to each other enough to seek forgiveness. That evening, we went to a celebration for a newly engaged couple on our staff team. As we were walking out of an ice cream store, the manager told the engaged couple that they ought to buy some guy's marriage videos she had seen advertised on television. This guy was Gary Smalley, she said, and his material would really help their marriage.

Norma smiled at me, slipped her arm around my waist, and jokingly whispered in my ear, "You ought to order those tapes."

2. Family Constitution

A second key to a long-lasting and satisfying marriage is to write a document that governs behavior for the husband, the wife, and the children—a family constitution.

We learned how to do this from Dr. Charles Shellenberger, our pediatrician at the time, and his wife, Dorothy. Later they became board members of my national ministry. Their constitution was the key to their own successful marriage and family harmony, and it became the basis for the disciplining and training of our children.

We had six articles in our first constitution. (We revised it from time to time as the children grew older.) In the first article, we agreed to learn everything we could about honor. Daily we would honor one another and honor God and His creation. As we reviewed it regularly with our kids, Norma and I were reminded that the single greatest thing we could do to enrich our marriage was to honor each other! For the children, the constitution spelled out consequences (no TV or having to do extra chores) for dishonoring behaviors.

When we agreed as a family on every part of the constitution, we all signed our names. This agreement became the "policeman" in our home. Norma and I were off the hook as enforcers—we could love and hug our kids even when they violated the contract, because the consequences had already been agreed to by them.

Eliminating anger as soon as possible was one article in the constitution that preserved marital harmony. "Before the sun went down," we had to seek forgiveness or give it. This promise kept wrath out of our marriage and out of relationships with our children. Fortunately, we never saw the teenage rebellion that so many families do. Such rebellion often comes from deep-seated resentment that you may not even know exists. Clearing out the anger and resentments daily and forgiving as often as it's needed will help to prevent explosions down the road.

3. Meaningful Communication

The third commitment that deepens marital love is developing a meaningful communication system that works for both partners.

How much meaningful communication does the *average* woman need? My own research indicates *about one hour a day*. Before any tongue-tied man panics, let me add that's *not* one hour *all at one time*. That's about 15 minutes in the morning as you're getting ready for work; five minutes on the phone from work; 20 minutes after work; 15 minutes once the kids are asleep; and five minutes before bed.

Our Best Method for Conflict Resolution: "Feather Talk"

After 30 years of marriage, Norma and I came up with a communication method that greatly increased our safety, security, honor, and love in those inevitable times of conflict. This tool can bring instant marital satisfaction and helps avoid the escalation and withdrawal that can lead to divorce.

According to historians, some American Indian tribes would resolve conflicts by gathering the leaders in a circle. One of the council members would hold a feather and explain all his thoughts and feelings on the particular conflict, while the others listened. When he felt they *understood* him, he passed the feather to another member, who then expressed his thoughts and feelings. The feather would make its way around the circle until everyone was heard *and* understood.

I learned this conflict-resolution method from my current mentors, Markman and Stanley, who call it the speaker-listener method. They advocate holding a card and I suggest a feather, but any object will do. The person with the object in hand has the sole purpose of being *understood*. The other person has the sole purpose of *understanding* what's being said.

The speaker expresses feelings and needs but avoids using the word *you* at all costs. Don't say, for example, "You make me feel . . ." as that can cause withdrawal or escalation. Try saying, "I feel like . . ." or "I need . . ." in short sentences. Your partner then repeats what she hears you saying, feeling, or needing.

Don't pass the feather to your mate until you have fully expressed your feelings and needs and your spouse understands you. But once that's done, hand over the feather and reverse the roles. And don't work toward solutions until *both* of you are completely satisfied that you've been understood. Depending on the severity of the conflict, you might need several hours or even a couple of days to think about it and then come back and review suggested solutions. But work at *understanding* each other first.

Here's an illustration of how this works. Michael and Amy are a young married couple. Amy is in charge of keeping the checkbook and paying the bills, and a conflict arose because Michael would sometimes use his bank ATM card to get cash and then forget to tell Amy or give her the receipt. As a result, her checkbook balance never agreed with the bank statement when it came at the end of the month, and that bothered her a great deal.

I asked them to try to work things out using the feather talk method, and Michael took the feather first. He started by trying to explain why he forgot to give Amy the receipts, and as the coach I had to gently pull him back to expressing feelings. Then he began, "I feel my forgetting to give you the receipts shouldn't be such a big deal that it causes a major conflict, as long as we can figure it out."

"So what you're saying is that you feel it's not a big deal if you forget the receipt," Amy said.

"No, I'm saying that my forgetting shouldn't lead to an argument that hurts my feelings or makes me feel like I'm being yelled at."

I clarified, "You're feeling hurt that she's really upset by it."

"Yeah, really upset by it," he affirmed.

"So you're saying you feel very hurt when I get upset at you for forgetting the receipts, knowing that you don't mean to do that," Amy echoed.

"Yes," Michael agreed.

Then he passed the feather to Amy. She started out with some accusatory *you* statements, so again as coach, I said, "Just share your feelings. How do you feel when he doesn't remember to give you the receipts?"

She tried again but was still really accusing Michael of irresponsibility. Then he tried to clarify. "I think what I hear you saying is you feel frustrated because you don't have all the tools you need to keep the finances up to exactly what they should be."

"That's right," she confirmed.

After they went back and forth a few more times, Michael repeated another of Amy's feelings: "I hear you saying you feel like you've failed if your numbers don't match up with the bank's numbers."

She agreed that was her feeling, and at that point they both felt understood. Then they brainstormed some possible solutions to the problem. Finally, they decided that he would try to get into the habit of giving her the receipt the same day he made a withdrawal, and if she didn't get any for a while, she would nicely ask him about it. The whole process took about 10 minutes.

The first time the Smalleys tried feather talk around the dinner table, we solved a nagging problem in 20 minutes, one that used to take two hours to discuss. The key point here is being understood. Once that takes place, then try to find an agreeable solution.

Don't take your partner for granted when doing this exercise. Even when Norma and I were getting in our hour per day of communication, there were times when she still didn't feel really understood at any point during the week. I went about my week assuming I understood her because we had talked. But it wasn't as meaningful to Norma because we didn't take the time to understand each other.

Daily communication and feather talk are particularly effective when used in conjunction with a fourth major strategy for protecting marriages, the support of a loving group of friends.

4. Group Support and Accountability

Small groups are vital to keeping marriages together. I've watched couples on the verge of divorce get involved in a support group and stay together. In all the years we've been leading small groups, we've never had one couple get a divorce (although some have come close). Sometimes we would stay up all night with angry couples trying to escape from the marriage. One time we paid for a wife's hospital stay when the couple was in financial straits. Another time we sent a person to a specialist in Colorado. Invariably, the troubled couple is greatly helped by the positive energy of people praying, caring, and accepting them. Also, all couples are strengthened weekly as they are held accountable for their family constitution.

A healthy small group accepts us for who we are. Even when we fail, we're loved in that context. We're regularly given new energy to continue resolving conflicts. And men learn best by watching how other men show love to their wives.

I encourage every couple to be part of a small, loving, healthy support group. I also urge men to form a small group with other men who will meet weekly to study the Bible and review their commitments. Otherwise, you'll be like a hot piece of coal that's pushed aside in the grill, becoming colder and colder until it dies alone in darkness.

I remember one man who balked at attending our weekly couples' meeting and receiving all the reminders. He just wasn't getting it. At one of our meetings, his wife confirmed that he wasn't communicating well or praising her. He was embarrassed and angered by her revelation. He stomped around and picked up his chair, turning it to face away from us. He told us to keep meeting but that he'd had enough. He felt like a failure and didn't want to continue.

I didn't know what to do, but a law professor in our group suddenly jumped out of his chair, fell prostrate on my living room rug, and started praying for the Lord to melt this man's heart and give him the courage to continue. I was so embarrassed and taken aback! But the dejected husband turned around and humbled himself, thanking the professor for praying for him. He recommitted himself to the group, saying, "One of these days, the Lord will help me make it."

That was more than 20 years ago. The man is still married and doing well, but it took two or three years for him to get his act together as a husband. Your growth as a husband and father will be unique to you, depending on your role models, your degree of unresolved anger, and your relationship with the Lord.

One last aspect of the power small groups can provide is a special version of this fourth commitment that Norma and I have used with great success. We call it our "911" group—three individuals who love us enough to be available to us at any time, night or day.

If Norma and I get into an argument that hasn't been solved that day, or if the subject we need to address is so sensitive that we're liable to get upset if we try to discuss it by ourselves, either of us can call "911." Twice this past year we've called this group of loving friends. They're like a court of appeals or a sounding board. Their presence and counsel bring safety, understanding, and calm assurances. Both times we dialed "911," we were able to resolve the outstanding conflict.

Although we speak to groups about what makes marriages work, Norma and I confess we don't live up to everything we teach every day. But at least we recognize when we're in trouble and rely on the Lord as our main source of power and love. We resolve anger as soon as we can—before the sun goes down. This keeps our relationship with Christ alive. We also commit to honor each other daily, and we keep learning and searching for more truth about marriage and family from God's Word and other resources. Years ago, when we first wrote out a family constitution, we set the course for a healthy family. This helped us keep our sanity and stay focused. We also take time for satisfying, meaningful communication. When we have serious conflicts, we use the feather-talk method to resolve them. And being in a loving support group holds us together as well.

These basic commitments have repeatedly saved our marriage, allowing our love to grow deeper over 30 years. I pray you, too, will find God's richest blessing on your life and in your marriage. As you do, your example of a loving, satisfying marriage will spread into your family and around your church and community.

Closing the Gap
by John Trent

You've finished reading the chapter "A Man and His Family," by Gary Smalley, which speaks about promise 4. Now it's time to complete the forms that follow. These are the Personal Evaluation form, where you give yourself an overall 1 to 10 rating on living out this promise; the Horizon Point form, where you sketch out a written picture of the man you would like to be three years from today; and three action points and potential barriers to fully living for Jesus in this area.

If you have questions about these forms, see the end of chapter 5, "A Man and His God."

Closing the Gap

4

**A PROMISE KEEPER
IS COMMITTED TO BUILDING A STRONG
MARRIAGE AND FAMILY**

Personal Evaluation Point

On a scale of 1 to 10, indicate by drawing a line where you stand in reference to promise 4. Then fill in the area below the line.

Setting a Prayerful Horizon

Lord willing, 3 years from now my life will reflect this promise in these ways:

My age today _____
3 years from today _____

10

5 - - - - - - -

1

_____
_____
_____
_____
_____
_____
_____
_____
_____
_____
_____
_____
_____
_____
_____

Closing the Gap

Action Plan Worksheet

Knowing that I need to improve in this commitment,
I will do my best to take a step of growth by following
through in the three areas listed below:

1. *Action Point*

_____

_____

Potential Barrier

_____

_____

2. *Action Point*

_____

_____

Potential Barrier

_____

_____

3. *Action Point*

_____

_____

Potential Barrier

_____

_____

Accountability Commitment

Who _____

When _____

Discussion Questions

1. Gary Smalley mentions several things that work against a man's ability to be successful in his marriage. Among them are a lack of training and a lack of mentors.

  a. Which of these has been the greatest hindrance in your marriage? Have you overcome it? If so, how? If not, what steps could you take to master it?

  b. Looking back, what do you wish you'd known before your marriage? How can you take what you've learned and pass it on to your children?

2. Take another look at the list of positive deposits and negative withdrawals in the chapter. Place a check mark next to each one that's a regular part of your marriage. Now total the number in each group. Are you running a deficit or a surplus? If the former, what changes do you need to make to get your account "in the black"?

  Show the results to your wife. Does she agree or disagree? Why?

3. Gary mentions that two signs your marriage is in trouble are the escalation of arguments and withdrawal. Is either of those going on regularly in your marriage? If so, what issues have caused those things to develop? How can you keep them from destroying your marriage?

4. Gary observes that unresolved anger is the great destroyer of relationships and that, at its heart, anger is a self-centered emotion we feel when reality falls short of our expectations.

  In the left-hand column below, list the things in your marriage that make you angry. In the right-hand column, list the expectation that's been unmet.

What Makes Me Angry	*The Unmet Expectation*
a.	a.
b.	b.
c.	c.
d.	d.
e.	e.

5. One of the best discoveries we can make about our anger is that it's our responsibility. Or, put another way, anger is a *decision* we make. Have two

guys in your group describe an experience that made them angry (it doesn't have to be something in their marriage). Then, as a group, analyze how a guy's feelings could be managed in that situation to prevent anger from taking hold. Use the following passages to guide your thoughts.

Proverbs 14:29; 15:1,18; 16:32; 19:11,19
Ecclesiastes 7:9
Ephesians 4:26,31
James 1:19-20

6. This chapter talks about four commitments that can make a marriage healthy. Of the four, which are you and your wife strongest in? Explain how that has strengthened your marriage. Which ones are you weakest in? How has that weakened your relationship? How can you shore up those areas?

A Man and His Church

by
Jesse Miranda

I learned early in life that the church is supposed to be much more than a handsome building or a pastor preaching in the pulpit. Where I grew up, the churches were the most beautiful buildings in the community, but that was about it. In spite of their beauty, they never seemed able or willing to meet anyone's practical, day-to-day needs. My father attended his church once or twice a year, and my mother took us on special holidays. As a result, I was never connected spiritually or physically to those church buildings. But I was connected from an early age to the *people* of God.

This began in a special way with an incident that occurred when I was three years old. A Christian couple came knocking on our door, asking to talk to my parents. My father was at work, and my mother was sick in bed. In fact, Mother was so sick that my sister, who was then five, and I had been caring for her for five days. The couple were warm and caring. There was something different about them that, even as a toddler, I could detect. They offered to pray for my mother, explaining that Jesus Christ was Lord, that He cared for us, and that He could even heal us. They prayed, and my mother was healed. Our family had never heard or seen anything like that before. This was my introduction to the good news of Jesus Christ. It was to

141

become my lifelong impression of the incredible blessing of God's people.

That episode taught me a valuable lesson: The ministry of God is done by the *people* of God, not just by ordained pastors. That means you and me—children, adults, new believers, laymen, and clergy alike. Scripture makes it clear that God intends for all those who call on the name of the Lord to be involved in His ministry. God easily could have called on His angels to fulfill His will on earth, but He chose you and me, as members of His church, to carry out His work. He designed it to be a highly personal calling according to the gifts He gave each one of us (see 1 Cor. 12:8-10). And the vehicle He provided for us to pour our gifts into is His church.

Spectator Christians Taking a Toll on the Church

As the twentieth century draws to a close, however, we're seeing a disturbing trend among God's people. Too many are relinquishing their awesome responsibility for sharing in God's ministry. They've elected to stand on the sidelines while the pastor runs the whole show. In a sense, by abdicating this priceless birthright, they have accepted something far less for their lives than God intended. Rather than exercising their God-given gifts, creativity, and labor to build up the church, they've become passive "pew-sitters." These marginal Christians are functionally distanced from the daily activity of the church and emotionally detached from the needs, pain, and often hopelessness their chronic indifference has bred among God's shepherds.

Sadly, we live in a spectator society, where Christians and unbelievers alike grow up watching life from the periphery, conditioned to hire something done rather than doing it themselves. Spectating, however, is not a luxury most pastors can afford. Without the daily support of dedicated servants, pastors today are running on empty. They're burning out at an unprecedented rate. God's chosen leaders are overworked, beaten up, stressed out, and ready, in many cases, to simply walk away from their life's calling.

To illustrate the point, I refer to a survey of pastors conducted by the Fuller Institute of Church Growth and reported by Dr. Arch Hart of Fuller Seminary in November 1991. It speaks to the loneliness, inadequacy, and stress many of our pastors privately experience every day.

- 90 percent work more than 46 hours per week, and often more than 60.
- 80 percent believe pastoral ministry is affecting their families negatively.

- 33 percent say, "Being in ministry is clearly a hazard to my family."
- 75 percent have reported a significant crisis due to stress at least once every five years in their ministry.
- 50 percent feel unable to meet the needs of the job.
- 90 percent feel they were not adequately trained to cope with the ministry demands placed on them.
- 40 percent report having a serious conflict with a parishioner at least once a month.
- 70 percent do not have someone they would consider a close friend.
- 37 percent have been involved in inappropriate sexual behavior with someone in the church.
- 70 percent have a lower self-image after they've pastored than when they started. (Wes Roberts, *Support Your Local Pastor*, 1995)

Can these possibly be the capable, courageous leaders we depend on to shepherd the church? Are these the people who committed their lives to serve God, minister in His Word, and pour themselves out as a drink offering to the glory of Jesus Christ? If so, what happened? And is it any wonder that God's purposes seem continually to be thwarted and many of our churches remain weak and sick?

Some might say, "Well, life's tough. We all have to work hard to survive, so quit complaining." But consider the pressures a typical pastor faces that are unique to the ministry. If the workloads of other professionals become heavy or unmanageable, they can simply refuse clients or refer them to another qualified expert. But most pastors don't feel the freedom to turn anyone away, regardless of how severely overworked they may be. Businessmen can postpone an appointment until they have a free slot in their schedules, but pastors (especially those without large staffs) are often on call 24 hours a day, *every* day.

Deeds Speak Louder Than Words

I will say it again and again: The ministry of the church is *our* ministry—yours and mine—not solely the pastor's. The spiritual battles our clergy face every day are incredible. The battles are intensified by well-meaning congregations that give thanks and praise with their lips, yet by their actions they make it clear they've lost respect for the pastoral position.

Our pastors need our loving support not just in word, but also in deed, or their chances of burning out—even failing—are enormous. Scripture urges us to honor and care for our pastors: "And now, friends, we ask you to honor those leaders who work so hard for you, who have been given the responsibility of urging and guiding you along in your obedience. Overwhelm them with appreciation and love!" (1 Thess. 5:12-13, *The Message*). True honor requires us to pour our hearts, energies, and resources into the lives and families of these dedicated servants. Are we each doing our part?

"Church" Means People, Not Buildings

As I've already mentioned, my earliest memories of church aren't of fine sanctuaries or cushioned pews. Once my mother got serious about church, "going to church" simply meant people meeting in one another's homes. It resembled Acts 2:46-47: "They broke bread in their homes and ate together with glad and sincere hearts, praising God and enjoying the favor of all the people." It was in this house church atmosphere that our family gathered with others to worship God and enjoy fellowship with our brothers and sisters in Jesus. I can remember hardly being able to wait to "have church."

Our family's house church eventually grew into a congregation that had its own building. It became organized and began to offer a variety of ministries. Our church was small, so everyone had to do his or her part to make it go.

In this supportive, nurturing atmosphere, I learned my earliest lessons in Christian servanthood. I learned, primarily, how important it is to honor and help one's pastor. My mother was my model in this. She was a housemaid and a cook, but she was also a faithful servant to the church. She served as the leader of the women's group and later became a "deaconess," one who would pray for and visit the sick. I also remember well how on Sunday mornings I would wake to the smell of delicious food. Mother was preparing our breakfast, but she was also cooking a large Sunday dinner. She would smile at me and say, "Today I'm inviting the pastor and his family over to eat."

As my family matured in the Lord, we learned to regard our pastors with the highest respect. We had several serve in the church in which I was raised. They were all different and possessed a diversity of gifts and qualifications, but they were all loved. They were looked upon as special men of God. They were our father figures, our counselors, our teachers, and friends of the family. They mentored me by showing an interest in me, and they kept me busy with church-related work. I was allowed to gain experience ministering in many ways. By the time I was 15, I was serving as Sunday school secretary; I also served in the youth department. At 17, I was assigned to a "preaching point," which today is known as church planting. While I was still a young man, I became a deacon of the church.

I came to hold the ministry in such high regard that I eventually spent 15 years teaching in a Bible school developing future pastors. Then I became a pastor's pastor—that is, a district superintendent. I continue to serve the leadership of the church as the associate dean at the School of Theology of Azusa Pacific University and a professor in the department of ministry, urging men and women to take up the mantle of leadership.

Because I learned to support and honor my pastor at an early age, I grew up loving the church. Because my childhood pastors taught me the importance of being actively involved in the life of the church, I have served it most of my life. This is the way God intended it. We worked alongside our pastors in the ministry, and they never felt isolated or inadequate. They knew we loved them by our *actions*.

Helping Our Pastors Find Their Way

In one of the "Peanuts" cartoons, poor Linus is standing in the middle of a weedy, unkempt baseball field. He's talking to himself, saying, "I don't mind playing right field. I don't mind standing out here in weeds over my head—if this is where I can do the team the most good. The only thing that bothers me," he concludes pitifully, "is that I don't know if I'm facing the right way."

That depicts the situation many pastors find themselves in today. Overworked, sometimes underpaid, under constant spiritual attack, many feel they're in over their heads. They're unable to discern if they're even facing the right way, much less ministering to the lost and hurting with power and authority. The challenges they face today are unlike any in history. Aside from the obvious pressures of trying to train and equip disciples in an age and culture where "church" is largely regarded as irrelevant, legalistic, and often hypocritical, there are many unseen stress-inducers that conspire to disarm and demoralize our pastors.

Consider that pastors, more than any other profession, are expected to be all things to all people. They're often exposed to unfair comparisons with other, higher-profile clergymen; they're expected to be models of righteousness and holiness; their families must be perfect; they're expected to meet the needs of everyone and have all the answers; they aren't allowed to have personal problems or marital conflicts; they can't get depressed; and they usually aren't given the leeway to simply be spiritually dry. Pastors are expected to be expert counselors, deft mediators, gifted financiers, and noble visionaries.

In the face of all these expectations, many have yet to find their vision for their ministry. I've spoken with many who are frustrated because they don't feel their everyday work touches the actual structures of life; they wonder if the church has moved to the periphery of people's lives. Their best efforts—their prayers, their studied sermons, their devotion, all their hard *work*—seem at best to address the *symptoms* rather than the *root* of people's problems.

John Aker compared ministry responsibilities to pins a juggler must constantly keep aloft. The minister has the pastoral task of visitation, the prophetic task of preparing and preaching sermons, the priestly task of planning and conducting services, the professional task of administration, and the personal task of developing his spirituality (Thomas Goodman, *The Intentional Minister*, p. 31).

This state of affairs we're discussing isn't restricted to the United States, either. Pastors all over the world face similar stresses, challenges, and outright attacks. They are hurting and in need of genuine friendship, prayer support, and affirmation for what they do. As men of God, we must step off the sidelines and get in the game, involving ourselves in the life of our churches. We do this most effectively by coming alongside our pastors with our service and daily prayers for their families, their marriages, and, most importantly, their continued growth in their relationship with Jesus.

Five Ways to Honor Your Pastor

Our family was poor, but we always gave honor and respect—and the gifts we could afford—to our pastors. Again, my mother set the example. I remember several times coming home from school and noticing that a rug was missing, some chairs were not in their usual place, or some other small items were gone. Instantly, I knew that the church had a new pastor who had moved into the parsonage. Mother had done some creative "housecleaning" on his behalf.

As a teenager, I came home from work one day to find that the first car I ever owned was gone. I asked Mother about my car, and she answered, "I noticed you've bought another car, so I gave your old one to the pastor. You're a single man and had two cars. The pastor has a wife and five children and only one car."

"But it was a good car," I argued.

"Yes," she responded, "I know. You should never give junk to the Lord."

Somewhat perplexed, I asked, "Why do you do so much for the pastors?"

"Son," she said, "I do for my pastors what I wish people will do for you someday, should the Lord call you into ministry."

That was a prophetic statement. I accepted a lifelong call to the ministry soon after. I also married into a pastor's family, the daughter of one of the pastors my mother blessed with her generous spirit. In turn, I reaped much of that same generosity. What my mother began turned into a wonderful legacy of blessing for God's appointed leaders.

Men, it's time for *us*—not just our wives or our mothers—to show the way in blessing and honoring our pastors. We're the men of the church, and God has given us the mantle of leadership. He has also given us the high calling of serving His shepherds.

In my travels and mission trips, I've asked dozens of pastors in churches large and small, denominational and independent, "What have men in your church done to honor you?" Many scratch their heads at such a question. But they're full of stories that reveal subtle ways they've been ignored or dishonored. We must begin to honor these men as the Bible instructs. Below are five ways you can support your own pastor.

1. Initiate a Relationship Without an Agenda.

One pastor recounted an experience that left him feeling used and confused. When he arrived at his first church, he was blessed by the invitations that poured in to treat him and his wife to dinner. He soon learned, however, that these gifts had strings attached. Person after person who called quickly betrayed that he wasn't interested in getting to know the pastor and his wife as friends but was pushing an agenda or making sure the new pastor heard his view on a personal or theological issue before someone else got to him.

If you're serious about honoring your pastor, spend time with him to build a relationship *without* an agenda. Make an appointment to see him and say, "I just wanted to come in and find out what I could pray for you about, and to see if there's anything I could do to encourage you." Support the pastor and his wife as people, not some authority to lobby to your own ends.

2. Provide Opportunities for Your Pastor to Bless His Family.

Another pastor I met was worried because he felt he was neglecting his family—especially his son. He arranged his schedule to spend all day with his boy one Saturday—and then the call came. A board member said he had tickets to a football game that same Saturday.

"Thank you," the pastor said, "I'd love to go, but I can't. I promised my son we'd spend the day together, and I need to keep my promise."

"You don't understand," the board member replied. "I'm not inviting you to go to the game with *me*. I've got two tickets so you and your son can go."

The board member had overheard the pastor expressing his need to spend time with his son, and he arranged for the tickets, as well as a team ball cap and shirt for the father and son.

Helping your pastor bless his family is a tangible way of honoring him. For instance, I know a pastor who has two daughters. Each Christmas season, a man in his church does something special. A few weeks before Christmas, he gives the pastor two crisp, new $20 bills—one for each daughter. But there's a stipulation: The girls must spend the money on a present for their mother. It has become a high point of the Christmas season, and all because someone takes the time and effort to help his pastor bless his family.

3. Be Specific in Praising His Ministry in Your Life.

A common complaint from pastors is how often a well-meaning parishioner will say, "That was a wonderful sermon, Pastor." But if asked, "What was it that specifically touched you?" the person gives blank stares and finally the empty response, "I guess I liked *everything* about it!" That response doesn't carry much weight.

Your pastor spends a lot of time in prayer and study for his messages. Being specific in your praise is a way of letting him know you were actively listening.

4. Be a Churchman, Not a Spectator.

Many people go to church today much as they go to the mall. They window-shop and browse, and their commitment to one "store" lasts only as long as they like what's being offered. If you want to honor your pastor, be a churchman, not a spectator. A churchman pitches in and helps in some capacity, attends services regularly, and supports the church financially.

5. Make Your Pastor and His Family a Key Part of Your Prayer List.

Have you ever told your pastor, "I'll pray for you this week," and then forgotten your promise until you saw him again the next Sunday? I know one man who remembers to pray for his pastor by setting the alarm on his watch for 4:00 P.M. each day. When the alarm sounds, wherever he is, he lifts his pastor in prayer. That gentle reminder puts teeth in his commitment.

Like a family member, your pastor needs and deserves your best in prayer. Your prayers not only support and protect him, but they also empower him to live out his challenging, high calling.

It's Time for Men to Set the Godly Example

Obviously, there are many other ways to bless your pastor and his family. My hope is that this chapter serves as a wake-up call to the men of the church. I pray it convicts us of our responsibility to our clergy and spurs our imaginations to new ways of expressing our appreciation. You and I have been placed in this world and given the gift of salvation to do ministry *with* our leaders.

We're not to bleed our pastors dry while we sit on the sidelines and cheer—or complain. We're not to engage them in relationships for our own benefit. Men of God must show the way; the time has come for us to set a godly example. If we acknowledge that the church is truly a body, it's clear that the pastor is but one appendage. Those of us who are the hands, feet, or legs can't forget to love, honor, and nourish those appointed as the head of the local church. We must each take personal responsibility for our commitment to our churches and pastors.

The church needs you. Your pastor needs you. And God calls you to meet those needs.

Closing the Gap
by John Trent

You've finished reading the chapter "A Man and His Church," by Jesse Miranda, which speaks about promise 5. Now it's time to complete the forms that follow. These are the Personal Evaluation form, where you give yourself an overall 1 to 10 rating on living out this promise; the Horizon Point form, where you sketch out a written picture of the man you would like to be three years from today; and three action points and potential barriers to fully living for Jesus in this area.

If you have questions about these forms, see the end of chapter 5, "A Man and His God."

Closing the Gap

5

A PROMISE KEEPER IS COMMITTED TO SUPPORTING THE MISSION OF THE CHURCH

Personal Evaluation Point

On a scale of 1 to 10, indicate by drawing a line where you stand in reference to promise 5. Then fill in the area below the line.

Setting a Prayerful Horizon

Lord willing, 3 years from now my life will reflect this promise in these ways:

My age today _____
3 years from today _____

10

5 - - - - - -

1

Closing the Gap

$$\boxed{5}$$

Action Plan Worksheet

Knowing that I need to improve in this commitment,
I will do my best to take a step of growth by following
through in the three areas listed below:

1. *Action Point*

_____

_____

Potential Barrier

_____

_____

2. *Action Point*

_____

_____

Potential Barrier

_____

_____

3. *Action Point*

_____

_____

Potential Barrier

_____

_____

Accountability Commitment

Who _____

When _____

Discussion Questions

1. Describe how you viewed church before you became a Christian.

2. How do you respond to the idea that we're all to be doing the work of ministry? Why? What might your service role be? Your financial role?

3. Jesse Miranda mentions that one of his memories is of his mother taking the children to church while his father worked. How would that affect a young boy's view of the church? Of his father? Of his mother?

If you can relate to Jesse's story, tell the group how your experience affected your view of the church.

4. How would you describe the world's view of a pastor? The average Christian's view? What *should* a Christian's view of a pastor be?

5. What are some creative ways you can express appreciation and support for your pastor? Brainstorm together, and write your ideas in the space below:

    a. _____

    b. _____

    c. _____

    d. _____

Make an agreement to put these ideas into action. Use the margins of this page (or another piece of paper) to write out that plan.

6. Pick a key player on your favorite sports team and think about what the team would be like if he decided to quit playing. What holes would it leave? What wouldn't get done that needed to be done? Believe it or not, each of us is a key player on his church team. If we're not in the game, some important things aren't getting done.

Talk with each other about what skills, spiritual gifts, and interests God has given you that you can use for the benefit of others and the glory of God. Write them below:

    a. _____

    b. _____

    c. _____

Now here's the challenge: If you're married, talk with your wife about how you can use the things above to benefit the church. Make a commitment to do so. Then, *before the week is out,* call your pastor, tell him of your interest, and ask how you can be involved.

A Man and His Brothers

by
John Perkins

*"One sign and wonder that alone can prove the power of the gospel is that
of reconciliation."*

—Vanney Samuels

Only by the grace of God do I not hate white people. And only by His grace
do I not go around the country telling my fellow black people why we
need to separate ourselves from the "white man."

Because I am a Christian, saved by the reconciling power of the gospel,
I'm compelled to allow Christ to live His life through me. And that means
that no matter what happened to me in the past, I must forgive and love.
Because He lives in me—only because of that fact—I *can* forgive those who
have treated me unjustly and learn to love even when I have often been
the object of others' hatred.

Reasons to Hate

Most black people believe they have reason to mistrust or even hate
whites. I have a little more reason than some. You see, I grew up in rural
Mississippi in the 1930s and '40s. All my major experiences with white people
gave me reason to get as far away from them as I could.

When I was only about nine, a black man accidentally ran over a white man. The black man was arrested and put in jail. Later that day, in the broad daylight of a busy Saturday, white men took him out of jail, tied him to the back of a car, and dragged him up and down Main Street until he was dead.

When I was 16, my older brother Clyde was gunned down by a white policeman. It was 1946, and Clyde had recently returned from Germany, where he had served our country during World War II. To many of us, he was a hero. He had been wounded in battle, which had won him a Purple Heart. But to the policeman who shot him, he was just another nigger.

The incident began as a minor disturbance one Saturday afternoon while we were waiting in line to see a movie. The box office was late in opening, and too many people were jammed into the small, hot alley leading to the theater's "colored" entrance. When some pushing and shoving broke out, a deputy marshal yelled, "You niggers quiet down!" He did not appreciate Clyde's defiant posture, so he tried to hit Clyde over the head with his nightstick. Instinctively, Clyde grabbed the stick, trying to protect himself.

That was too much for the deputy to handle. He took a couple of steps backward, shot Clyde twice in the stomach at point-blank range, then turned around and left. For all he cared, Clyde could lie there and bleed to death. A few hours later, after my cousin and I rushed him to the hospital, Clyde was, indeed, gone. And for what?

I could easily tell these stories as a way to demonstrate why we black people need not have anything to do with white people. For many of us, the wounds seem much too deep, and the least little scrape can peel off the scab and expose the painful sore. White Christians need to understand that these painful injuries make men like Louis Farrakhan appealing to some African Americans.

But that's not the reason I tell stories from the past. For me they demonstrate the power of the gospel to reconcile people no matter how much they've been alienated from each other. These stories are also a reminder that we should not take reconciliation for granted. It won't come automatically just because we say we want it. We'll have to work for it.

Reconciliation should never become a fad—something we think we can deal with one time and then move on to something else. The history of the tattered relationship between blacks and whites in this country (and between other races as well) has deep roots and will not be healed by chopping down the tree in one fell swoop. For me, only the love of Christ could reach beneath the surface and replace bitterness with love.

The event that helped me begin to see the necessity of racial reconciliation took place long before the O.J. Simpson verdict showed so vividly how differently blacks and whites look at the world. It was the horrible night of February 7, 1970. I tell this story not to dredge up the past unnecessarily or to point a finger at anybody, but rather to show the reconciling power of God.

The fight for economic and racial justice in rural Mississippi landed me and 19 others in the Rankin County jail that night. It was the longest and most horrible night of my life. Determined to teach us a lesson, white law enforcement officers, including state troopers, beat and tortured us for most of the night. I honestly thought they were going to kill us.

Because of my faith in God, I was not afraid to die, although I certainly didn't want to leave my family. And when I saw the hatred playing on their faces, I knew those men wanted us to suffer before they killed us. I did not want to suffer.

Sheriff Edwards was in my face almost as soon as I was through the door, yelling about how I was a "smart nigger" but that I was not safe because I wasn't in Simpson County anymore. They knew how to treat "smart niggers" in Rankin County.

"This is a whole new ball game, nigger!" he shouted. "How do you like this, nigger?"

All the while he was yelling at me, he was hitting me with his fists. I had to resist my natural tendency to fight back, because I knew they would certainly shoot me if I did—the same way they had killed my brother Clyde so many years before.

Throughout the night, they kicked and beat us mercilessly in the side, the head, the groin. They used fists and leather blackjacks, often five big, strong men at a time pummeling one of us. After they had pounded us into unconsciousness, they would wait until we revived and then start in on us again.

I don't know how many times I drifted in and out of consciousness that night. I only know that the beating and kicking seemed to go on forever and that the pain was excruciating. I also remember that the first thing I would see, whenever I came to, was lots of blood all over the floor, and I knew that most of it was mine. I knew I wasn't the only one being brutalized, and I wondered if they had killed anyone yet.

Not only were they beating me and my dear friend Curry Brown, but they were also beating some of the college students who were with us. Sometime during the night, they shaved Doug Huemmer's head and beard and poured moonshine whiskey all over him. (Doug was a white friend and co-worker.) Then they did the same to Curry.

Those men—men sworn to protect and serve the public—were having a party. All during the time they were beating us, they were walking among us drinking moonshine out of paper cups. The more they drank, the more creative they got with their violence. (I'm sure the moonshine gave them the idea of shaving Doug's head.)

At some time during this long, terrible evening, they began to scream at me because I was bleeding on their floor. "Hey, nigger," one of them said, "what are you doing bleeding all over my floor like this? Hey, Ralph, you see what this nigger done to our floor?"

"Why, that's disgusting," the other man replied, having hilarious fun at my expense. "You just get up right now and clean up this mess!"

They brought me a mop and bucket and forced me to start cleaning the floor, even though I was so weak and in so much pain that I was afraid I would pass out at any moment. Then they continued to punch, slap, and kick me because I wasn't doing a good enough job to suit them.

From what they were saying, I gathered that they thought some FBI agents were on their way to check out the situation. That's why they wanted the blood cleaned away and why they ordered me, once the mopping was finished, to go into a bathroom and wash up. If they thought washing my face would hide the evidence of the horrible beating I had taken, however, they were wrong. Soap and water couldn't disguise the cuts, bruises, or swelling.

Unfortunately, the FBI never showed up, which only made our captors even angrier. One of them came over to me and put a gun to my head. "I think I'm gonna kill me a nigger!" he announced.

He pressed the cold steel hard against me, and I knew the end had come. Slowly, he squeezed the trigger.

Click.

The chamber was empty. It was just another way for a man with a badge to have some fun. They had a good laugh about it and then beat me into unconsciousness yet again.

By the time I regained consciousness, they had thought of another vicious game to play. Someone had brought in a list of the demands made by the black citizens of Mendenhall, and they thought it would be interesting to hear me read the demands out loud while they hit and kicked me for emphasis. By this time my head was hurting so badly that I could barely see well enough to read, and my throat was so sore that I couldn't speak much above a whisper.

"Nigger, read louder!" one of them demanded.

"I just hate a nigger who won't speak up," someone else snickered.

"Hey, nigger, I didn't quite get that demand of yours," said another. "Why don't you read it again so I'll know exactly what you want us white folks to do for you?"

I don't know how long this went on. I don't know how I lived through it. I had only one source of comfort—the fact that the Son of God Himself knew exactly what I was going through, because He had been treated the same way, and He was without sin. I tried my best to hang on to that thought, though I have to admit it wasn't always easy.

Finally—I don't know why—they decided they had done enough for the night, and the beatings stopped. Maybe they were getting tired, or maybe they wanted to stop just short of killing us. But mercifully, we were booked, fingerprinted, and taken upstairs to our cells.

It's strange, I know, but lying in the cell with every part of my body hurting, I began to feel pity for the men who had beaten me. I thought about what hate had done to them, turning them into brutal, unthinking savages. I thought about those faces twisted into unreasoning, snarling, hideous things, and I shivered.

I remembered how, the night I was in jail in Mendenhall a few weeks earlier, Lloyd "Goon" Jones, a state trooper, had been trying to stop rumors that we were being beaten inside the jail. "Now really," he had said to Vera Mae, my wife, "do you think I'd do something like that?"

Vera Mae's reply had been, "Yes, I do."

Jones had pretended to be shocked and hurt by her answer. But that night of February 7, stomping and kicking me with every bit of his strength, he had proved she was right. Hate had done that to him.

I'm sure that some of the guys who brutalized us so terribly thought of themselves as good family men. They loved their wives and were gentle to their children and kind to their parents. But hate is a demon, and it destroys men's souls.

I was determined that it would not destroy my soul. I didn't want to be like those men. I didn't want to hate back. In fact, I knew I couldn't hate those men. God's love would not let me hate anyone for any reason.

After we were all released on bail a few days later, when doctors examined me, they found that the beatings I had sustained had done a lot of damage to my stomach, which led to two different surgeries.

It was hard when Vera Mae brought the children to the hospital to see me after the first surgery that immediately followed the beating. That was almost more than I could bear. I remember specifically the reactions of two of my children.

Derek, who was just a little guy, threw himself on the foot of my bed and sobbed, it hurt him so badly to see what they had done to his daddy.

Joanie, who was 14, just went stiff. She couldn't stand it and had to leave the room. Vera Mae followed her outside and tried to comfort her, but Joanie didn't want to be comforted. With tears in her eyes and anger in her voice, she told her mother, "I will never, ever like a white person again! I mean it. I hate them!"

Joanie was wrong. She was able to overcome her anger and bitterness against white people, although she says she still struggles sometimes.

For me, that long, horrible night in jail began to open my eyes to what racism had done to white people. Before that incident, I would have said blacks were the only victims of racism. But an interesting thing happened to me that night. When I looked into the distorted faces of those men, who seemed more like demons than humans beings, I couldn't hate them back. What I felt, apart from the consuming fear, was pity for those men. They, too, were victims of the sin of racism, because it had twisted them to the point that they could beat and kick us as if we were animals and feel no remorse.

That night I tried to bargain with God. I prayed that if He would let me live and get out of that jail, I would preach a gospel that was bigger and stronger than my race—a gospel that would break down the barriers of race.

Although I came close to dying that night, God answered my prayers. For nearly a year, I struggled with the promise I had made to Him. I also had trouble believing that a loving God could allow something like that to happen. Many of those men who beat me called themselves Christians, and if they could be Christians, maybe I needed to be something else.

The injuries I sustained that night landed me in the hospital again. I had to have two-thirds of my stomach removed, and not long after, I suffered a heart attack. As I lay in the hospital bed following that, I thought back to my conversion to Christianity. God had used a Presbyterian minister to disciple me in the Word. That old white man taught me the Scriptures and believed in me, convincing me that God was going to use me in spite of my self-doubt.

The Spirit of God worked on me as I lay in that bed. This Jesus I had preached, did He really understand what it was like to be a black man in Mississippi? How could He understand what I was going through? But then an image formed in my mind, an image of the cross. This Jesus knew what I had suffered. He understood and cared, because He had experienced it all Himself.

This Jesus, this one who had brought good news directly from God in heaven, had lived what He preached. Yet He was arrested and falsely accused. Like me, He went through an unjust trial. He also faced a lynch mob and was beaten. But even more than that, He was nailed to that cross and killed like a common criminal.

At that crucial moment, it seemed to Jesus that even God Himself had deserted Him. The suffering was great. But when He looked at that mob who had lynched Him, He didn't hate them. He loved them. He forgave them. And He prayed, "Father forgive these people, for they don't know what they're doing."

His enemies hated, but Jesus forgave. I couldn't get away from that. The Spirit of God kept working on me and in me until I could say with Jesus, "I forgive them, too."

Returning Love for Hate

God took an incident that was meant for evil and used it for good. His love began to take from my soul every bit of anger and hatred. I knew there was no way I could keep that love from overflowing to the people around me. White people, black people, any other kind of people—it didn't matter. I experienced a second conversion while I lay in that hospital bed, a conversion to love and forgiveness.

In the more than 25 years since that time, I have dedicated my life to reconciliation. God has given me the chance to speak to thousands of people, especially Christians, from across the country, convicting and encouraging them to move beyond their comfort zones and make a genuine effort to confess their racism, build new friendships, and make a commitment to loving each other beyond any barriers of race and culture. I believe this kind of deep, reconciling love demonstrates the power of the gospel to the world.

Maybe even more important to me than that opportunity is the friends God has brought into my life. I think of Roland Hinz, a white businessman I met in 1983. Roland has become my dear brother. I can share anything on my mind with him. We challenge each other, encourage each other, and receive one another in love. Roland stood with me through the development of Harambee Christian Family Center in Pasadena, California; he stood with me through the creation of *Urban Family* magazine in 1992. He has been a faithful friend, and I love him dearly.

God has also brought many more dear friends into my life. I think of Wayne Gordon, a white brother who has worked so hard for more than 20 years in Chicago's inner city. We became close friends in 1977, and since that time we've shared the joys and pains of doing Christian community development in the inner city. I think of the continual support and friendship I receive from Malcolm Street, Steve Lazarian, Jeff Cotter, Roy Rogers, and others.

Returning love for hate, embracing my white brothers, and pursuing reconciliation has provided such a deep joy and purpose. As we stand together as blacks, whites, Asians, Hispanics, and Native Americans, we will recognize that Christ has *one* church, and the love that flows from that truth will ignite the flame that can burn away the walls dividing us.

I am greatly encouraged by the movement we're beginning to see toward racial reconciliation. I'm enthusiastic about Promise Keepers making racial reconciliation and the discipleship of men across all boundaries a core principle of its mission. Coach McCartney has been courageous in his commitment to this cause.

In addition, InterVarsity Christian Fellowship, the National Association of Evangelicals, the National Black Evangelical Association, and the Christian Community Development Association (CCDA) movement, among others, have been doing some wonderful things in this area. Many in the charismatic movement have made racial reconciliation a similar priority. All these committed efforts are thrilling to see.

Reconciliation may be the new revival. When the Body of Christ is unified, God's Spirit will be poured out. Racial reconciliation is a chance to demonstrate the unity of the Body of Christ to the world. Without this unity, we will be presenting a truncated gospel forced into our own cultural boxes. So let's look at how we, as individual Christians, can help to make reconciliation more of a reality.

What Can I Do?

You may remember what Edmund Burke said—that the only thing necessary for evil to triumph is for good men to do nothing. As Americans and as Christians, all of us should feel compelled to do what we can to help bring healing between the races. But there are questions: What can I do? Where can I start? Can I really make a difference? The answers to those questions, respectively, are *plenty; right where you are;* and *yes, you can.*

Specifically, there are six things you must do if you want to be an instrument of racial reconciliation. These are the same six things I've learned and tried to practice in my own life over the past 25-plus years.

1. Acknowledge the existence of the problem and the way it affects you.
2. Confess your own guilt.
3. Seek God's guidance.
4. Be willing to take risks.
5. Discover opportunities for action.
6. Move beyond saying hello.

Let's look at each of those in turn.

1. Acknowledge the existence of the problem and the way it affects you. One of the biggest reasons we haven't dealt effectively with alienation between races in this country is that most of us just don't see it. It so surrounds us, and we've put up with it for so long, that it seems normal and we just don't see how it affects us.

The first of the 12 steps of Alcoholics Anonymous is to acknowledge the existence of the problem (in their case, that the person is an alcoholic). In the same way, we cannot overcome racial divisions without acknowledging that they exist and that we've all been tainted by racism.

Remember the words of Isaiah: "Woe to me! . . . I am ruined! For I am a man of unclean lips, and I live among a people of unclean lips" (Isa. 6:5). Our paraphrase might be: "Woe to me, for I am ruined! I am a person with racist attitudes, and I live among a people of racist attitudes."

Can we ignore the continuing reality of racism and pretend that everything is as it should be? Absolutely not! The love of Christ compels us to work for change. If you're ready to admit there is a real problem in this country, you've taken a big first step toward the elimination of the problem.

2. *Confess your own guilt.* If you're a Christian, you know you're a sinner. The Bible is clear on that point. And I would dare say that if we examine our lives closely enough, most of us can find ways in which we have sinned by perpetuating racial division. These are personal sins with which we must deal.

Even if a close examination of your life fails to turn up anything, it's still appropriate to confess the guilt of our fathers. You see, there are personal sins and there are societal sins. Societal sins have produced the racial strife and violence in this country. Anyone who wants to see our country healed must be willing, as Daniel and Nehemiah were, to help shoulder the load of our society's sins.

It grieves me that this country has never officially repented of her past sin of slavery. But complete healing cannot be brought about by an act or proclamation of the government. It can be accomplished only through individuals—people like you and me. Are you willing to help bear the burden and shame that racial division has brought to this country? Are you willing to let God break your heart over our society's sins of slavery and bigotry and men mistreating other men because their skin is either too light or too dark? If you are, God will use you as a minister of peace and healing.

If you're not, then before you can change anything else, you'll have to change yourself. But God is available to help in that, too. If you as a black person think that all whites are arrogant and condescending, spend time praying about it, and see if God doesn't bring someone into your life who is just the opposite—someone who will help you overcome your prejudice.

3. *Seek God's guidance.* Prayer is the preparation for ministry, but a lot of Christians have the wrong idea about prayer. They think it only means talking to God, but it also involves *listening* to God—listening expectantly for Him to speak to our hearts.

Ask God what He wants you to do, and expect Him to answer. Ask Him sincerely. And keep on asking until you get His answer. While you're at it, ask Him for the strength and wisdom to accomplish the task He gives you to do.

Let God show you areas in your community where you can help to bring about reconciliation. Ask Him to reveal areas where you need to grow or areas where you have a special gift for service. You may not feel like an expert, but if you're yielded to God, He will use you as a peacemaker. And remember what Christ said: "Blessed are the peacemakers, for they will be called sons of God" (Matt. 5:9).

4. *Be willing to take risks.* It isn't easy to be a risk taker, especially in a world that often gives itself over to negativity and hate. But it helps a lot if you remember two things:

Love is stronger than hate.

Light is stronger than darkness.

If you're armed with the love and light of God, no enemy anywhere can stand against you. And the more risks you take, the stronger and more sure of this you will become.

A risk doesn't have to be a big thing like going into south-central Los Angeles to talk to the Crips and Bloods about Jesus Christ. That might be a risk God would call you to take, but for most men, His call is more likely to be to something smaller, though in its own way just as significant. I'm talking about being willing to be rejected or humiliated in order to build a bridge to someone of another race. Should I try to be your friend, or will you reject me because I'm black—or white? If I'm afraid of being rejected, I'll never take the risk and the bridge will never get built.

Again, the best advice I can give you about taking risks is to start small. Don't feel bad about that. Wherever you're starting, it's a launching pad for bigger and more noteworthy accomplishments in the future. The important thing is to start somewhere. Then, as God gives you more courage and strength, be willing to step out in faith and take risks of greater magnitude.

One good place to start is simply to introduce yourself to someone of another color or ethnic background and try to cultivate a friendship. As I travel around the country, I see that there is little social interaction among the races—quite a bit less, in fact, than there was 10 years ago. The Berlin Wall was torn down within the last few years, but the wall of separation between the races in America has grown higher than ever. Risking rejection by saying hello to a member of another race is a good way to start putting some cracks in that wall.

5. *Discover opportunities for action.* If you keep your eyes open, you'll discover opportunities for action. After you've prayed about it and made your-

self ready to take risks, just walk around your community and talk to people, and you'll begin to find out what the needs are.

In your community, there's a need that only you can fill, and if you don't fill it, the world will be poorer as a result. So will you, because you'll have missed something important. Benjamin Mays, who served for years as president of Morehouse College, often reminded his students of this truth, and many great men and women who came out of that school (including Martin Luther King Jr.) grabbed the opportunities for service that came their way.

Here are some specific ways you can look for opportunities to be an instrument of reconciliation:

- Educate yourself about the issues. By reading this book, you're already on your way. In addition, in the last few years, several books have been written on this subject from a Christian perspective.

- Visit an inner-city church. For the most part, integration has meant that minorities could join white churches. But that has always put the burden on minority people to step outside their comfort zone. Visiting a black or Hispanic church is a good way to become more comfortable with differences. And who knows—God may lead you into a life-changing friendship with a brother from another race or culture.

- Help create environments where cross-cultural relationships can develop. Organize a mission trip from your church to an inner-city ministry. Such trips are excellent for broadening people's vision for reconciliation. These outings are often billed as service trips but turn into much more.

- Work with inner-city children in your community. Getting involved with local kids is a great way to build bridges of trust. But do it out of genuine Christian love. While children are always hungry for more involvement in their lives, they can spot people who have the wrong motivations, like guilt or pity. And remember, such work is a long-term commitment.

When Vera Mae and I first moved with our children back to California, we started working with a few of the kids in our neighborhood. We made it clear that we were determined to build a better future for them—even though the neighborhood had the highest daytime crime rate of any neighborhood in the U.S. That meant providing day care and Bible clubs for the youngsters. It also meant putting our lives on the line in order to drive out the drug dealers and gangsters who were destroying the kids' lives. Today, we work with hundreds of children every day, and although our neighborhood is far from perfect, it has come a long way from what it was just a few years ago.

Keep your eyes and ears open. Opportunities for service are all around you.

6. *Move beyond saying hello.* Merely saying hello to a person of another race or ethnic background is a big step for some people. But it's only the first step. If that's where you leave it, you haven't accomplished much. It's important for whites, blacks, and Hispanics to get to know each other, to engage in serious dialogue. Believe me, that's not always easy. People of color are often suspicious of whites, and it may take some effort to get beyond that suspicion. Sometimes whites are motivated more by guilt than by a genuine interest in a person of another race as a human being. That, too, may be difficult to overcome.

Okay, we might as well face it: Sometimes, even though they may not mean to, white people have feelings of superiority that express themselves in a condescending attitude, and that can be a source of friction. Some blacks have these feelings of superiority, too—or we have feelings of inferiority that push us in the direction of defensiveness, resentment, and bitterness. Such attitude problems really get in the way when two people are trying to develop an honest, open friendship. It may take a lot of love and patience to move beyond saying hello, *but it will be worth it.*

The racial problems in this country and throughout the world will not be solved without a lot of hard work. It's past time that we in the church take this mission of racial reconciliation seriously. *If our Christianity doesn't have enough power to tear down walls of separation, why should the unbelieving world choose our gospel over any other religion?*

The legacy of racism, racial tension, and separation offers Christians a unique opportunity—the chance to rise above the pretenders. The more we're able to cross the boundaries between groups of people, the more proof we have to offer the world of the truth of our gospel. And the more our Christianity can present a Body not divided like the rest of the world, the louder we will be able to say with conviction that Jesus is, indeed, the answer.

Closing the Gap
by John Trent

You've finished reading the chapter "A Man and His Brothers," by John Perkins, which speaks about promise 6. Now it's time to complete the forms that follow. These are the Personal Evaluation form, where you give yourself an overall 1 to 10 rating on living out this promise; the Horizon Point form, where you sketch out a written picture of the man you would like to be three years from today; and three action points and potential barriers to fully living for Jesus in this area.

If you have questions about these forms, see the end of chapter 5, "A Man and His God."

Closing the Gap

6

A PROMISE KEEPER
IS COMMITTED TO DEMONSTRATING
BIBLICAL UNITY

Personal Evaluation Point

On a scale of 1 to 10, indicate by drawing a line where you stand in reference to promise 6. Then fill in the area below the line.

Setting a Prayerful Horizon

Lord willing, 3 years from now my life will reflect this promise in these ways:

My age today _____
3 years from today _____

10
5
1

Closing the Gap

Action Plan Worksheet

Knowing that I need to improve in this commitment,
I will do my best to take a step of growth by following
through in the three areas listed below:

1. *Action Point*

_____

_____

Potential Barrier

_____

_____

2. *Action Point*

_____

_____

Potential Barrier

_____

_____

3. *Action Point*

_____

_____

Potential Barrier

_____

_____

Accountability Commitment

Who   _____

When   _____

Discussion Questions

1. Reread the account of John Perkins's beating in Rankin County, Mississippi. If that had happened to you, how would you have felt about the men who beat you? Why? How would you have felt when your children saw you after stomach surgery?

2. John talks about how God's love for the men who beat him overpowered any hatred that could have taken root. How did you feel as you read that section?

3. John also says of that night, "God took an incident that was meant for evil and used it for good." How do John's experience and perspective compare with those of Joseph in the Bible? (See Gen. 37–50, especially 50:20.)

Describe an instance in your own life when someone did something that was intended as evil, but God turned it into something good. How has that experience affected your faith?

4. This chapter suggests there are six things each of us can do to bring racial healing to our country. Go back and review each one. Then, as a group, talk about these questions:

   a. Which of these areas is my biggest blind spot? Why?
   b. What risks am I willing to take in the next month to build bridges with people of other races or denominations?
   c. What's the best way for me to find resources to help build those bridges?
   d. What people of different races do I know at work, in my neighborhood, and at church? What steps can I take to build relationships with them? Use the space below to record ideas:

Name	What I can do to build a relationship
1.	1.
2.	2.
3.	3.

Hold each other accountable to the ideas you've listed.

A Man and His World

by
Luis Palau

What one man has most influenced your life? A friend? A relative? A pastor?

The man who most influenced me I haven't seen now for more than 50 years. But the example of my father's fervent love for God and heartfelt concern for others has stayed with me all these years since his death.

Even when, as a teenager, I was tempted to walk far away from the Lord, I couldn't bring myself to disgrace my father and everything he stood for. At age 17, after four troubled years torn between two worlds, I finally made an all-out commitment to God in heaven. I didn't express it as articulately as this, but in essence I said, "With your enabling, Lord, I promise to influence my world for Your glory by obeying the Great Commandment and the Great Commission in every area of my life."

Just like my dad, I wanted to become a man of integrity, a man of influence bringing blessing to my family, my friends, my community, and my world for God's glory. I gained a vision for winning people to Jesus Christ and urging believers to go on for Him all the days of their lives.

Thank God, He has answered that prayer. Despite my imperfections, which are many, and my natural tendency to try to do things in my own strength, which is futile, He has used me to urge many to get right with Him. He has given me a sphere of ministry beyond my wildest dreams.

Have you ever dreamed how God might use you to influence your world for His glory—I mean, really *dreamed?*

If not, ask yourself, "Have I made an all-out commitment to Jesus Christ yet? Is He truly the king of my life?" And if you haven't made that commitment, I urge you to do it now, before you continue reading this chapter. Whether you're young or old, tell God: "With Your enabling, Lord, I, _____ (insert your name), promise to influence my world for Your glory by obeying the Great Commandment and the Great Commission in every area of my life."

You may be thinking, *But Luis, I've already committed my life to the Lord. And frankly, I still don't feel like a man of influence. In my home, I'm less than effective. Outside the home, it's even tougher.*

On the authority of Scripture, however, I guarantee that God is more than able and willing to grant you the power to become a man of tremendous influence in your world, for His glory.

It's yours for the taking.

Sometimes I've had to learn this truth the hard way. For example, I once lived next door to a young television personality. We would chat from time to time, and he mentioned that he listened to my radio program occasionally. But I didn't present the gospel to him. *He seems completely immune to the problems of life,* I thought. He was a playboy type who lived "the good life." He didn't seem to care about spiritual values at all.

This neighbor eventually married a bright college graduate. After his wedding, everything still seemed to be going great for him. He and his wife would leave for work together, laughing and talking.

Suddenly, though, he changed. The joy seemed to have left his face. He and his wife started driving separate cars to work. I could tell their marriage was souring, and I felt the need to talk to him, but still I didn't want to meddle in his life. I went about my business and headed off for a crusade in Peru.

When I returned home, I learned that my neighbor had killed himself. I was heartbroken. I knew I should have gone to him and urged him to repent and follow Jesus. But because of false courtesy—because I followed a social norm—I never did it.

Though my neighbor seemed carefree, his soul was hurting, and I'm sure he would have welcomed the Good News. From that experience, I learned not to allow politeness to keep me from telling others about Jesus.

The Power of God's Love

God promises to give you and me the life-changing power of love, a love that transforms everyone we know and meet. Are you willing to grab hold of this power in your own life?

It's not an issue of availability; it's a matter of obedience to the Great Commandment: "Love the Lord your God with all your heart and with all your soul and with all your mind and with all your strength" and "Love your neighbor as yourself" (Mark 12:30-31).

When all is said and done, the fulfillment of God's law is a matter of love (see Gal. 5:14). The greatest Christian virtue is love (see 1 Cor. 13). The fruit of the Spirit is summed up in one word, *love* (see Gal. 5:22). The very character of God is love (see 1 John 4:8, 16). Above all else, we're commanded to "put on love" (Col. 3:14).

By nature, however, most of us are unloving and, frankly, often unlovable. Only as we experience God's love and reciprocate by loving Him can we truly love others regardless of race, religion, gender, or geography. And when we love them this way, people will be willing—even eager—to listen to our presentation of the gospel.

The world doesn't understand this kind of love. It doesn't even know what it means. The word *love* is one of the most misunderstood, misappropriated terms in any language.

What matters to God is this: Are you willing to take hold of the power of God's love and let it transform your life and relationships? If you're serious about obeying the Great Commandment, you're automatically saying yes to God's will and no to the vices of the world, the flesh, and the devil.

It's your choice.

The Power of Jesus' Gospel

God also promises to give you and me the life-changing power of the gospel, which is "the power of God for the salvation of everyone who believes" (Rom. 1:16).

It's the Good News that "God so loved the world that he gave his one and only Son, that whoever believes in him shall not perish but have eternal life" (John 3:16).

It's the revelation that "Christ died for our sins according to the Scriptures, that he was buried, that he was raised on the third day according to the Scriptures, and that he appeared to Peter, and then to the Twelve. After that, he appeared to more than five hundred of the brothers at the same time" (1 Cor. 15:3-6).

After His resurrection, right before His ascension, Jesus declared: "All authority [power] in heaven and on earth has been given to me" (Matt. 28:18). In other words, He's King of kings and Lord of lords. Whatever He says, goes.

"Therefore go and make disciples of all nations, baptizing them in the name of the Father and of the Son and of the Holy Spirit, and teaching them to obey everything I have commanded you" (Matt. 28:19-20a). That's His Great Commission to us.

But the Lord hasn't given us such a great responsibility without also giving us the power and authority we need to get the job done: "And surely I am with you always, to the very end of the age" (Matt. 28:20b). By His indwelling of us and universal availability to others, we have the power to proclaim His gospel in our homes and among our relatives and friends so that others may believe, repent, and be saved.

Have you taken hold of the power of the gospel? Has it taken hold of you? Your family? All those nearest and dearest to you?

The Gospels tell us that Christ came "to seek and to save what was lost" (Luke 19:10). Indeed, as evangelist Clyde Dupin has said, "There is nothing more important to God than rescuing what He created."

Analyzing what's wrong with America is laudable and necessary. Teaching how to live rightly in this mixed-up world is commendable and true. But unless we communicate the life-changing gospel of Jesus Christ and call people to conversion, we invariably help perpetuate the crises at hand. Both Scripture and history bear out this truth: *Without a wave of conversions, it's impossible to change a community or nation for good.*

I don't care how many billions of dollars the government spends on education and reform; true change is a matter of the heart. And outside of the gospel of Jesus Christ, you can't change your own heart, let alone truly influence others for good.

Oh that God would give you and me a passion for those who have yet to commit their lives to Jesus Christ and experience the transforming power of His gospel! If we're serious about seeking to influence our world for God's glory, we need to be shaken into action by the reality of what Scripture teaches about hell and the destiny of those who reject Jesus Christ.

Love Your Unsaved Wife to Jesus
Man, does your wife love Jesus with all her heart? If you're not sure, how can you rest? How can you possibly even be interested in outside activities? How can you bear to leave her side if you have no assurance she knows the Savior and has eternal life?

The other day, I talked with a man in Grand Rapids, Michigan, who has known Jesus for years, but his wife didn't. For 13 years, he loved and prayed for her, and during one of our recent evangelistic crusades, she finally came to the Lord. I had an opportunity to visit with this couple not long ago. You could see the sense of joy and relief on his face. Now, at last, God's love is shed abroad in both of their hearts. They're on the same path, confident of God's blessing in this life and the next.

Love Your Prodigal Children to Christ
Man, have your children come to Christ yet? If not, by the power of the gospel, please, no matter how long it takes, do all you can to love them to the Savior.

One story in particular was an encouragement to me long before my own prodigal son came back to the Savior. It involved a young Australian soccer star who was totally caught up in his sport, chasing women, and making the bar scene. Yet he always knew there must be more to life. Finally, at one of our London crusades, he decided to get serious about Jesus Christ. Afterward he said, "That night, this prodigal son's life was turned around. I'm so glad to be finally 'back home,' part of God's forever family."

There's no greater joy than when your prodigal child comes home. Andrew is my third of four sons, born in Cali, Colombia, in 1966 while my wife, Pat, and I were first-term missionaries. After graduating from the University of Oregon, Andrew moved to Boston, where as a confident young man he began his climb up the corporate ladder. But it wasn't his distance from home that troubled my heart; it was his distance from the Lord.

Like our other sons, Andrew had prayed to invite Jesus into his heart when he was a child. Since high school, however, he had shown little interest in the Bible and church. Fraternity life ruled in college, where Andrew followed the path of least resistance. God occasionally stepped in but could not fit in.

Now living on the other side of the continent, Andrew kept a secular lifestyle with secular values. Painful as it was, Pat and I had to accept what we had counseled other parents. Just because Andrew was brought up in Sunday school, had memorized Scripture verses, was baptized, could talk the language, and even respected and defended the gospel as truth—all that didn't mean he was truly converted. Conversion is essential for everyone, whether born into a pagan family or one that seeks to honor God.

Pat has always been blunt. Regarding Andrew she said, "If your child reaches adolescence and does not spontaneously follow Christ, perhaps he isn't a Christian." Jesus said the proof is in the fruit. A parent who says "My son is a Christian, though right now he's not living the life" may be doing the child a disservice. Andrew was extremely respectful to us, always courteous and kind, a tremendous son who never blasphemed the gospel. But his life denied a personal conversion experience with the Lord Jesus Christ.

So often, during our evangelistic crusades, as I sat on the platform and prayed, "Lord, may many come forward to confess Christ," at that same moment I'd be thinking, *There's no greater joy than this . . . but what about Andrew? How can my joy be complete until Andrew stands here as one who walks with Jesus?*

An element of sadness permeated my life. And I realized that if my heart carried this weight, God's heart was far more sad, because His love is so much more selfless and pure. This truth is at the heart of Jesus' assertion in the Sermon on the Mount, "If you, then, though you are evil, know how to give good gifts to your children, how much more will your Father in heaven give good gifts to those who ask him!" (Matt. 7:11).

Andrew's rebellion was a painful lesson. Because one of my sons, whom I did my best to channel in the ways of Jesus, resisted conversion, I was kept from certain aspects of arrogance and from self-righteousness. The gospel is all of mercy, all of grace. I was not so charming and wonderful as to cause Andrew to walk as a saint and never besmirch the Lord's name. I could do no more than cling to God's promise to Israel: "All your sons will be taught by the LORD, and great will be your children's peace" (Isa. 54:13). I prayed that verse many times through the years for all my sons.

Finally, just a few years ago, Andrew returned to the Lord. Pat and I had invited him to come with us to Jamaica for the "Say Yes to Jesus" crusade in February. There he met Robert Levy, the crusade's finance chairman, his son Chris, and his daughter Wendy. Their energetic commitment to Jesus convicted Andrew of his harmful waywardness. Though his good intentions to change subsequently failed, weeks later another visit to Jamaica (to see Wendy) led to what Andrew calls "some serious repenting."

Was it first-time repentance and genuine belief? Was it a recommitment to Christ? To me it doesn't matter when my son was converted—as a child or at age 27. My joy is that now both of us, all glory to God, know the Spirit of God is living in him. Andrew is born of God and bearing the fruit of sonship, being conformed to the likeness of the Lord Jesus Christ. His enthusiasm for the things of God is one of the greatest joys of my heart.

Every child in a Christian family makes his or her own choices, of course. That's what makes loving a prodigal son or daughter so hard. But if any of your children don't know the Lord yet, please, love them to the Savior.

Love Your Parents and Other Close Relatives to Christ

Man, are your parents and other close relatives part of God's family, or do they still know nothing of His grace and mercy? If the latter is true, never give up. Ask God to bring other Christians into their lives, and do all you can to show your love and concern.

A friend of mine, Bob, was burdened about his 70-year-old father's eternal destiny. "Luis, what am I going to do?" he asked. "I hardly ever see him. He lives 2,000 miles away. But as far as I know, he's never given his life to the Savior."

Some time later, I called Bob. "How's your dad doing?" I asked. "I've just been invited to preach in his city."

Even though he had other commitments, Bob immediately made plans to fly back east, invite his dad out for dinner, take him to the crusade where I was preaching, then fly out of town the next morning.

After the crusade meeting that night, Bob and his dad met me at a nearby hotel for dessert. I asked Bob's dad, "Mr. Bobosky, have you given your life to Jesus?"

He said yes.

"When did you do it?"

"Tonight," he said. "You twisted my arm."

I put my arms around him and said, "Well, Mr. Bobosky, I'm glad I twisted your arm."

Actually, Bob did all the "arm-twisting." All I did was have the privilege of proclaiming God's Good News in a setting where Mr. Bobosky could hear the message, be touched by the Holy Spirit, and commit his life to Jesus Christ.

If your mom and dad still haven't come to Jesus, pray for them. Plead with God for their salvation. Ask Him to use you and other Christians in their lives. And do anything and everything you can to see they hear the gospel and are encouraged to put their trust in the Savior. "Compel them to come in" (Luke 14:23, NKJV).

Love Your Distant Relatives to Christ

Man, what about your distant relatives? Keep them in your prayers, too. If you don't care whether they come to Christ, who will?

Take advantage of extended family reunions, vacations in cities where you have relatives, and business trips to reconnect with distant relatives. Even if you've never met before, call them up. Get together. And take the opportunity (maybe your only chance in this life) to tell them about the Lord.

When my travels took me to Barcelona, Spain, recently, I seized the opportunity to visit the town of L'Escala. It's a picturesque seaside resort community, and my father was born there eight years before his family emigrated to Argentina. Today, more than 200 Palaus and Parnaus (my paternal grandmother's family) call L'Escala home, out of a population of 5,000.

After we arrived in L'Escala, the mayor invited my family and me to a festive luncheon attended by many of my long-lost relatives. At that luncheon and afterward while touring the area, I invited everyone to attend a gospel rally scheduled later that same day. Many came that night, and a number gave their lives to Jesus.

Even if you talk about the Lord with only one long-lost relative on your next trip, won't it be worth the time and effort to go out of your way to see that second cousin, that great-aunt, or that brother of your grandmother who may not yet know the Savior?

Love Your Neighbors to Jesus

Next to your family, your neighborhood is the nearest part of your world, and sometimes no less of a challenge. It's convenient to make excuses for not persuading our neighbors to follow Jesus Christ. We don't want to be overbearing or offensive.

That's the mistake I made with the neighbor whose story I told earlier. I followed the social norm of false courtesy, of avoiding hard or controversial topics of conversation, and as a result—to my great sorrow—I never challenged him to trust in Jesus as his Savior.

When we approach life's situations with the absolute conviction that we're to tell others about Jesus, however, we'll have the courage we need. We'll discover that people are open to the gospel message.

Love Your Friends to Christ

Even if your wife, children, parents, and other relatives all love the Savior, everyone has at least five friends or acquaintances who need the Lord. Think about it. Whom do you know who still needs Jesus? Anyone you meet more than once is someone about whom you should wonder, *Does he or she know the Savior?*

Just because someone goes to church, don't assume he has committed his life to Jesus Christ. I talked with two friends recently, Wayne and Wain. Both have gone to church virtually all their lives. Both love to sing in their respective church choirs; both are near retirement age; and both volunteered to sing in our crusade choir. But it wasn't until the last day of the crusade, when Wayne stood to go counsel someone at the invitation, that Wain took his arm and said, "Why don't you just stay right here and counsel me?"

Conversely, just because some of your older friends have rejected Jesus all their lives, never give up hope. Herb served as finance chairman for our most recent crusade in Texas. Even though he was eager to see many people in East Texas come to the Savior, in his heart he had to pray, "Lord, I don't want to go to heaven without my best friends."

Herb had a lengthy list of people for whom he was praying, but he kept three men's names at the top. All three had known Herb for 15 to 25 years but had always put off surrendering to the Lord. Finally, during the crusade, two of Herb's three close friends trusted the Lord. A few days earlier, the other friend also gave his life to the Lord, in his own home, when Herb stopped by for a visit.

"I had many other friends who gave their lives to Christ during the crusade, some I brought and some who told me a few weeks later," Herb said. "But it's so good to know for certain that those three closest friends finally are believers."

Never Give Up

Another man I know, Mike, took our evangelistic association's "Bridgebuilder" friendship evangelism training and gained a vision for how the Lord could use him to win his friends to Jesus. In particular, he had a burden for a co-worker named Wes, a rough, abrasive fellow.

Mike started having coffee with Wes, who made it clear he didn't need God or anyone else. This went on for a while until the day Wes was carried out of work on a stretcher and rushed to a nearby hospital. Doctors discovered his heart had doubled in size and other vital organs were shutting down. They gave him less than a year to live.

As soon as Wes got out of the hospital, Mike went to see him. Mike took Wes through the plan of salvation. "He agreed with everything I was saying," Mike told me later. "We even went through the prayer of commitment." But Wes put him off.

So Mike went back through the gospel basics. Wes still said no thanks. When Mike finally got up to leave, however, Wes said, "Wait, tell it to me again," and a few minutes later he gave his life to Jesus.

Mike and Wes ended up talking another couple of hours that night. Since then, Wes has joined Mike's church and become an outgoing witness for the Lord. "He's a real encouragement to the believers at work as well as the unsaved," says Mike. "They keep saying, 'What's happened to Wes? He's so happy. Doesn't he know he has less than a year to live?'"

You don't have to be a promise keeper for 25 years before you start witnessing for Jesus. A member of my evangelistic association, Dan Owens, is one of the most effective young evangelists I know. His father didn't come to Jesus until his thirties and doesn't happen to be an outgoing public speaker like Dan. As a hard-working construction man, however, Richard has led more than 90 other men to Jesus since the early 1970s!

Whether you have the gift of evangelism or not (Dr. C. Peter Wagner estimates 15 percent of all believers do), the Lord calls us all to help fulfill His Great Commission in our generation. It's not always easy, I admit.

I remember a major crusade we had in the capital city of one country. The president invited me to meet him, go to his church, and then talk one on one about the Christian faith. I immediately accepted his invitation. As far as I knew, no one had ever witnessed to this man before.

After my initial excitement wore off, though, I began to worry about what others would say if I went to his particular church. Some pastors confirmed my fear. I knew what the Lord would have me do, but I turned coward. I backed out at the last minute, asking the presidential chauffeur to give my apologies to the president.

Immediately after the driver left, I realized what a mistake I'd made. My joy was gone. That afternoon, I prayed, "Lord, forgive me. I'll never turn down another opportunity to witness to somebody because I fear what others might think."

You may not have a chance to speak with the president of the United States. But what about the CEO of your company? Maybe he's aloof. Critical. Abrupt. Almost inaccessible. Nevertheless, pray for him. Do your best. Strive for excellence. Gain a good reputation. And then, when the opportunity comes, ask him about his soul. Give him a New Testament, a gospel booklet, or an evangelistic cassette.

Better yet, invite your boss, your co-workers, and other unsaved friends to the next Promise Keepers conference. You can be sure the gospel will be proclaimed and an invitation will be given for them to trust Jesus. Thank God, multiplied thousands already have come to Jesus on the opening night of Promise Keepers conferences around the country!

God's Power in Our Lives

To keep our promise "to influence my world for Your glory by obeying the Great Commandment and the Great Commission in every area of my life," we need the Great Condition. What's that, you ask? It's this: "Be filled with the Spirit" (Eph. 5:18). It's this: "Be filled to the measure of all the fullness of God" (Eph. 3:19). It's this: "Christ lives in me" (Gal. 2:20).

This divine, revealed truth is the very heart of the New Testament. This is what the "new" is all about. It's no longer God in heaven and we men here on earth. Ever since Jesus went back to heaven and sent His Holy Spirit, God literally indwells us. "Don't you know that you yourselves are God's temple and that God's Spirit lives in you?" (1 Cor. 3:16).

This truth so permeates the New Testament that we take it for granted and miss the reality of what God is telling us. If I may paraphrase, He's saying, "Listen, man, apart from Me you can do nothing. In fact, if I don't indwell you, you have no part in Me. When you open your heart to Jesus, I come in and take up permanent residence within you. It's no longer you alone, struggling on your own, but 'Christ in me.'"

This truth absolutely revolutionized my life and ministry when God finally impressed it upon my heart during my graduate school days. During a 20-minute chapel talk by Major Ian Thomas (founder of the internationally acclaimed Capernwray Bible Schools), while I was at what is now Multnomah Biblical Seminary, I finally learned what "Christ in me" means.

It doesn't simply mean that I now identify myself as a Christian.

It doesn't mean that Jesus is with me in some mystical, spiritual sense.

It means that the Lord Himself literally indwells me.

From the opening pages of Matthew's Gospel all the way through to the end of Revelation, the Lord is trying to tell us, "What's 'new' is that I am now choosing to live in and through you to win the people of this world, which I've made, for My glory."

It's not our love, our gospel that's going to change anyone's life. It's God's love, God's Good News of salvation. And it's only by His love in and through us, communicating His gospel message, that men, women, youth, and children will be saved.

You're not convinced? I challenge you to read through the New Testament with a pen or highlighter in hand. Mark every verse you find about God indwelling believers. You'll be astounded at what you discover.

What's the secret of being a promise keeper, a man of integrity who's influencing his world for God's glory? It's not us, doing our own little thing, in our own power. It's God at work in and through us. And it's the power of God's Word, quoted by heart whenever we have an opportunity to tell others about Jesus.

Imagine what the world will be like if you and I join hands with millions of other brothers in Christ (and sisters, too) and promise to stay true to God's Great Commandment and Great Commission for the rest of our lives! We'll witness the greatest "season of refreshing" in all history!

A Word of Caution

As promise keepers, whenever we dream and plan and pray about influencing our world for God's glory, we need to keep in mind that God's timing is often different from ours. The problems in our family, our community, our city, and our nation don't just spring up. They're the result of years, decades, even centuries of sin, disobedience, frustration, and neglect. We can't change everything overnight, nor should we secretly wish we could change things that fast.

God isn't the author of chaos and confusion. While He calls us to be men of action, there's a time and place for everything. Let's not get ahead of the Lord.

Realistically, it takes at least half a generation before someone's conversion has any impact on society. Often, it takes a generation and a half. Church history bears that out. Just look at the great revival sparked by John Wesley, for instance. A massive wave of conversions transformed England from bottom to top. Even the worst of that nation's social vices were rooted out—but it didn't happen overnight. It didn't all happen even in Wesley's lifetime; slavery wasn't abolished until a few years later. But even secular historians admit it was Wesley's influence on Christian politician and reformer William Wilberforce that eventually won the day.

Too often, we greatly *overestimate* what we can do in a year and greatly *underestimate* what, by God's enabling, we can do in five, 10, 15, or 25 years, let alone 50.

I'm thrilled at all God has done through the Promise Keepers movement the past five years. But what is this talk in certain circles about whether this is as good as it's going to get?

What cynicism! What unbelief! How such talk must grieve the Lord's heart! I'm not alone in saying I believe God is about to do something over the next few years far greater than anything we can think or imagine.

May we never get so worried about the ups and downs of the moment that we lose sight of God's overall plan and purpose for our own generation—and the generation to come.

"Be faithful, even to the point of death, and I will give you a crown of life" (Rev. 2:10). Let's take the risk of going all out for God and leave the results to Him.

Closing the Gap
by John Trent

You've finished reading the chapter "A Man and His World," by Luis Palau, which speaks about promise 7. Now it's time to complete the forms that follow. These are the Personal Evaluation form, where you give yourself an overall 1 to 10 rating on living out this promise; the Horizon Point form, where you sketch out a written picture of the man you would like to be three years from today; and three action points and potential barriers to fully living for Jesus in this area.

If you have questions about these forms, see the end of chapter 5, "A Man and His God."

Closing the Gap

7

A PROMISE KEEPER
IS COMMITTED TO INFLUENCING
HIS WORLD

Personal Evaluation Point

On a scale of 1 to 10, indicate by drawing a line where you stand in reference to promise 7. Then fill in the area below the line.

Setting a Prayerful Horizon

Lord willing, 3 years from now my life will reflect this promise in these ways:

My age today   _____
3 years from today _____

10

5

1

_____
_____
_____
_____
_____
_____
_____
_____
_____
_____
_____
_____
_____
_____
_____
_____

Closing the Gap

$$\boxed{7}$$

Action Plan Worksheet

Knowing that I need to improve in this commitment,
I will do my best to take a step of growth by following
through in the three areas listed below:

1. *Action Point*

_____

_____

Potential Barrier

_____

_____

2. *Action Point*

_____

_____

Potential Barrier

_____

_____

3. *Action Point*

_____

_____

Potential Barrier

_____

_____

Accountability Commitment

Who _____

When _____

Discussion Questions

1. Think about the following statement individually, then discuss how each of you filled in the blank:

"The one thing that characterizes God more than anything else is

_____."

Why did you answer the way you did? What does 1 John 4:7-8 say about the issue?

2. If God is love and our job in life is to reflect His character, our mission is to let people know what love looks like. On a scale of 1 to 5, 1 being "not well" and 5 being "very well," how would you rate yourself on showing God's love to your . . .

	Score	A practical thing I can do is:
Wife?		
Children?		
Those in authority?		
Friends?		
Co-workers?		
Nation's leaders?		

What's one practical thing you can do to move your score closer to a 5 in each area? Use the second column for your answers.

3. Luis Palau talks about the power of the gospel to transform lives. Yet we can sometimes be afraid to talk about it with nonbelievers. Why is that?

Now read Romans 1:16. If each of us were to really take what Paul says to heart, how would it change (a) our view of the gospel and (b) how we feel about discussing it with other people?

4. Luis also talks about key relationships in our lives that may involve an unbeliever. Talk through the following questions with the guys in your group.

    a. Which people are you most concerned about? Why?

    b. When was the last time you tried to present the gospel to them? How did it go? What roadblocks did you run into?

    c. Choose three people in your life who do not know Jesus. With the help of your group's accountability, make a commitment to do these things:

        • Pray at least three times per week that God would give you an opportunity to talk with them.

- Pursue opportunities to spend time with them, praying that God will use one of them to open the door for the gospel.
- When God presents that opportunity, *take it*.

Special Note: If you're a little rusty on how to present the gospel, make plans to talk with a pastor or someone who's gifted as an evangelist about how to do it.

5. At the beginning of the chapter, Luis says, "Whether you're young or old, tell the Lord:

With your enabling, Lord, I _____ (insert your name), promise to influence my world for Your glory by obeying the Great Commandment and Great Commission in every area of my life."

That's kind of scary, isn't it? Talk about what scares you most about making this promise. Then pray the prayer with the guys in your group. As you do, keep in mind that God never calls you to do something He won't *enable* you to accomplish. So trust that—and be a part of the most exciting, dynamic work in the world.

Synthesis, Cycles, and Stepping Out

by
John Trent

Congratulations! You've now worked through this book, taking a hard look at each promise area. Using input from your small group and spouse, you've developed a basic plan of action for living out each promise. All this will help you move toward your personal horizon point and prayerfully move toward greater Christlikeness.

But now that you've got all the individual parts of your Closing the Gap plan, how do you put them into an easily understandable format? I suggest you take a tip from a well-known mouse.

Standing in the Center of Your Life Story

While the current Disney Corporation has done certain film projects that mock biblical values, that wasn't true of its founder. In 1929, Walt Disney and a small team of talented animators were hard at work on Disney's first "family friendly" animated cartoon. It was a black-and-white creation called "Steamboat Willie," and it introduced the world to its favorite rodent, Mickey Mouse. At the time, the French were the leading animators, having cartoon characters that stood stock still on film, with their mouths opening and closing. Disney had other plans for Mickey.

He wanted the irrepressible star of his cartoon to be full of life and fun. That meant not only that his mouth would have to move, but he'd also be breathing in and out, turning the ship's wheel back and forth, and tapping his foot while he whistled a happy tune. All this action, plus that of other characters for Mickey to interact with, would make his story "come to life."

Today we take such animated realism for granted. However, in 1929, it was a spectacular achievement. That's because for that much character movement to take place, hundreds upon hundreds of individual art cells had to be drawn and sequenced together. And that's where the problem—and the solution we'll adapt for our own purpose—came in.

In the late 1920s, computer technology as we know it didn't exist. Instead of having sophisticated programs to help generate artwork, each and every cell had to be individually hand drawn. (By contrast, the Disney film *The Lion King* uses more than 2.4 million individual cells, but computers greatly aided in the creative and duplication process.) Walt Disney soon had so many individual "pieces" to his story that it was becoming incredibly difficult to keep track of where he was in the process. In other words, he couldn't see the forest for all the trees!

That's when Disney recalled the work of another creative genius, Leonardo da Vinci, and adapted a technique da Vinci devised that allowed him to arrange many pieces into a single, overall picture. Today, the concept is called *storyboarding*, and it's used by creative teams and individuals from the Pentagon to Madison Avenue. (I describe storyboarding in more detail in my book *LifeMapping*.) For Disney, it allowed him to move from confusion to creating a masterpiece.

In a small warehouse in Southern California, Disney took all the individual pieces (art cells) of his story and hung them sequentially on the walls of the room. That way, by standing in the center of that room, Disney or any of the other animators could look around and see how the entire story, from beginning to end, was coming—*and much more than that.*

An old axiom says, "The sum of the parts is greater than the whole." In other words, once you can see all the individual parts of a story—*or in our case a plan of action*—you can see more than just random pieces. You gain an overall picture that begs to be modified as needed. That's just what Disney did to create his first Academy Award winner, and that's also what you can do to compile a "winning" plan of action.

Compiling Your Personal Evaluation and Action Points

To begin putting the pieces of your growth plan into an overall visual display, fill out the Life Perspective sheet that follows. Simply take all seven of your personal evaluation points at the end of chapters 5-11 and list them on this chart. Then connect the lines, and you'll have a graph that can tell you in a single glance which promise areas have the greatest gaps you need to narrow.

As you transfer your personal scores to this sheet, time-date this first overall look at your current walk of faith. That will give you a baseline, or starting point, for where you are today. At the end of your small-group experience, *and then again at six-month intervals thereafter,* update this sheet to see how you're doing at closing each gap. (Some may want to use one color of ink to draw their initial graph, then a different color at a later point as a time-dating method.)

Again, please remember that whatever your initial Life Perspective sheet looks like, every man is in process. From the apostle Paul himself to the newest believer in Jesus, all of us have gaps that won't be totally closed until we see Him face to face. Whether you're looking at several or few scores below the midline, we all have room for growth in godliness. The important thing is what you're committed to doing—living out your plan and closing those gaps.

Now you'll utilize the Disney method mentioned above to take the action items you compiled at the end of each chapter and put them into a single visual display. On the form on pages 196-97 labeled "Moving Toward Christlikeness," write out each action item and potential barrier. Again, please note that this initial plan is your best effort to design a prayed-over set of goals and directions. It's important to keep this plan in pencil as it remains flexible to God's leading. Action items and potential barriers can and often will change as you seek to close the gap over the long haul. Keep in mind that your plan, like your heart, needs to be soft toward God, not chiseled in stone.

As you'll notice, your Moving Toward Christlikeness summary sheet is actually a storyboard of your personal goals and potential barriers. By gathering all the parts of your plan in one place, instead of being overwhelmed or confused, you can clearly consolidate your plan.

Closing the Gap
Life Perspective

1	2	3	4	5	6	7
A Promise Keeper is committed to honoring Christ.	A Promise Keeper is committed to pursuing vital relationships with other men.	A Promise Keeper is committed to practicing integrity.	A Promise Keeper is committed to building a strong marriage and family.	A Promise Keeper is committed to supporting the mission of the church.	A Promise Keeper is committed to demonstrating biblical unity.	A Promise Keeper is committed to influencing his world.

Now with your plan completed and captured on paper, it's time to prayer-fully put it into action. To do so, we encourage you to pour it through a series of life-changing seven-week growth cycles.

"Standing on the Promises..."
Your Group and Seven-Week Growth Cycles

As we mentioned in chapter 3, a centerpiece of the Closing the Gap plan is having small groups meet in a series of "growth cycles." To further explain the purpose and function of these cycles, let's pull a hypothetical group together and see how these imaginary friends employed them.

Jim, John, Jeff, and Joe are men of different backgrounds, professions, and races who all attend the same church. They were little more than casual acquaintances until last summer. That's when they all boarded a bus from Phoenix to Los Angeles to attend a Promise Keepers stadium event. During the drive there and back, and especially at the conference itself, they formed a close-knit bond that has lasted all year. Since the conference, they've gotten together socially with their wives and even joined the same Sunday morning couples class. That's where they heard of this book and, after much discussion, committed to meet together as an encouragement and accountability group.

They First Develop Their Plan in Cycle One

Their first cycle of eight weeks began by discussing their Personal History sheets and then working through each promise area—just as you have. They would read each chapter and evaluate and fill out their personal evaluation points, action points, and potential barriers. Then in their eighth week together, they talked about and prayed over their overall Life Perspective and Moving Toward Christlikeness sheets, followed by a time of praise and worshiping God. This eighth week of "rest" ended the first cycle and left them with a completed plan of action they prayerfully set out to apply.

Putting First Things First: The Goal of Cycle Two

Now that their basic plan was outlined, it was time to "own" the items written down. To turn their plan into habit patterns, not just hoped-for changes, they began a second cycle of seven weeks. For the first six weeks of this cycle, they would focus on just one promise, actively seeking to live out their first action point and confront their first potential barrier in the first two weeks, their second action point and potential barrier in the next two

Moving Toward

	1	**2**	**3**
Seven Promises	A Promise Keeper is committed to honoring Christ.	A Promise Keeper is committed to pursuing vital relationships with other men.	A Promise Keeper is committed to practicing integrity.
1. *Action Point*			
Potential Barrier			
2. *Action Point*			
Potential Barrier			
3. *Action Point*			
Potential Barrier			
Accountability Commitment			

Christlikeness

4

> A Promise Keeper is committed to building a strong marriage and family.

5

> A Promise Keeper is committed to supporting the mission of the church.

6

> A Promise Keeper is committed to demonstrating biblical unity.

7

> A Promise Keeper is committed to influencing his world.

weeks, and their third action point and potential barrier in the final two weeks.

For example, let's suppose our group decided to start with promise 4. This promise focusing on loving his wife and family presented Jim's greatest gap. He was a new Christian whose marriage had been on rocky ground for some time and needed immediate attention.

While Jim had been trying every day to be more of God's leader and lover in his home, for the next six weeks, he was going to make a special effort in this area. As you can see below, Jim's first action point item was to "actively listen to my wife instead of cutting her off." That had come directly from a pointed talk with his wife during the development of his plan. "I need you to *listen* to me," she'd told him. "I'm tired of saying the same things over and over and feeling like you never hear me."

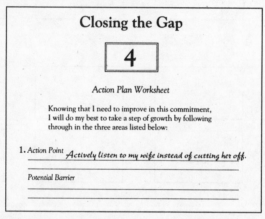

Closing the Gap

4

Action Plan Worksheet

Knowing that I need to improve in this commitment,
I will do my best to take a step of growth by following
through in the three areas listed below:

1. *Action Point* *Actively listen to my wife instead of cutting her off.*

Potential Barrier

Jim had already described this first action point to his small group of friends, so when they met together that first week, John, Jeff, and Joe had all been praying the same thing for him, and all had the same question: "How'd you do at listening to your wife this week?"

Jim said honestly that it had been a difficult challenge to try to reverse years of blocking out her words. But with the goal of being a better husband in mind, he had tried looking her in the eye as they talked (a suggestion given by Jeff in their group time). And he'd made sure he put down his paper whenever his wife asked him a question (a suggestion he'd gotten from Joe). It hadn't been a perfect week by any means, but his wife had said she could see him making efforts in that area, and it encouraged her—*and him*—a great deal.

Jim was also asked by the other men how he had done at facing the first potential barrier he'd listed on his plan. As you can see below, that was "Face how poorly my parents (esp. father) listened to each other."

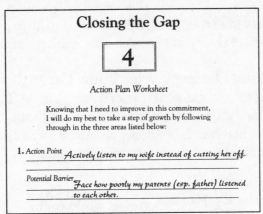

Jim had never been one for looking back at the past. Yet he'd made a commitment to confront his number-one barrier in this promise area. To do that, he determined that he needed to face the dynamics of his father's style of relating to his mother, to see how it related to his own. As part of confronting this barrier, he had made a call to his mother, and they had a rare talk about her and "Daddy's" communication. What he learned from her was that he'd gotten his lack of listening skills honestly. His father and grandfather had both hidden at work and behind the newspaper instead of really communicating and listening.

Jim reported his insights to his group and asked them to pray that God would help him confront this generations-old barrier. The verse Jim claimed was Philippians 4:13: "I can do all things through Him who strengthens me" (NASB).

As you can see through this hypothetical example, the second cycle calls for individual prayer and action, blended with a spouse's and small group's support. This process was followed by each man in the group for the first six weeks. Then, during the seventh week, they all rested and used their meeting time to praise God for what He'd done in their lives, to ask for prayer, and to revise individual parts of their plans as needed. In their third growth cycle, they repeated the process, this time focusing on the number-two promise on their priority list.

For men with strong personal disciplines, their group could end after three growth cycles (or at least their study of this book). They outlined their plan the first eight weeks, and they "practiced" it by putting it into action (with the help of loving support) during the second and third cycles. Now they could individually cycle through the remaining five promises. However, many men would benefit from continuing to meet for up to five more growth cycles to see all the parts of their plans become daily habit patterns.

Meeting During Cycles Four Through Eight

The purpose of these additional cycles is easy to grasp. The pattern of six weeks of "work" and then a time of "rest" is repeated. During the fourth cycle, you focus on your number-three priority promise. During cycle five, you give attention to your number-four priority promise, and so on.

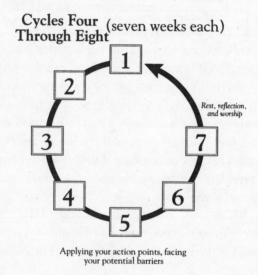

Cycles Four Through Eight (seven weeks each)

Rest, reflection, and worship

Applying your action points, facing
your potential barriers

A person usually needs to do something for at least 21 days in a row before it becomes a habit. By the end of your fourth cycle, you'll have worked at your plan for more than 200 days! And you'll have spent focused time for 29 weeks seeking to live out the seven promises and overcome potential barriers.

If your group has continued for four cycles, you may want to keep your group together and study another book or do a book study in the Scriptures (while continuing to work on your plan individually). However, some groups may want to complete eight full cycles, covering all seven promises. Again, in the week of rest that concludes each cycle, you'll be encouraged to reflect, revise, pray over, and amend your original plan of action and potential barriers. That's what keeps your plan targeted and specific to what God's teaching you—what keeps you going the distance and closing the gap.

If your group decides to go through all eight cycles, counting holidays and weekends, that's more than a *year* of working toward being God's man. And while a year of focusing with a small group of friends on living out these promises is great, it may be time for you to buckle your chin strap and use what you've learned to help someone else develop his own Closing the Gap plan.

Time to Jump

Why should you consider stepping out of a perfectly good small group? The answer is clear: *God calls us to a ministry of multiplication.* We're to "grow and go," not "sit and soak." So ask yourself, "Who do I know that would really benefit from going through this same process?" Maybe it's someone at church, at work, or in your neighborhood. Perhaps you have a son who's old enough. Once you've identified an individual or group of guys, we challenge you to take a major step of faith and guide them through the process you've just completed.

We know some men simply aren't spiritually or relationally in a position to lead others. But don't just grab for the safe option. If you're not ready to lead on your own, team up with a brother in your group, and the two of you co-lead. That way, as an apprentice or co-leader, you can still gain the experience and heightened commitment that come from leading, not just listening.

"But I'm just an ordinary Joe!" you might say. So are the rest of us. But there's nothing ordinary about the God within you. We know it's going to be incredibly hard for some men to trust the Lord and move toward a mentoring position in other men's lives—but we need you. Remember, desiring to be a godly leader is an "honorable thing" in God's eyes, and it's a desperately needed role in the lives of many men.

You've now been given a call to brokenness, seen and identified potential barriers to spiritual and personal growth, worked hard to develop a plan of action, and been challenged to cycle those godly goals into your own life. Then we've asked you to start the process all over again as a mentor and see other men's lives change as well. We know this is a big challenge—but we also know Who can provide the courage and strength to finish the journey.

A Final Word to "Pilgrims" Beginning a Long Journey

Listen to the words of an old, old story. It's the story of a pilgrim who had already walked many miles and yet had far to go before reaching his final destination—a bright, shining "City on a Hill." On the road, the pilgrim walked with staff in hand, tired, yet steadily trudging onward. Suddenly, an angel of God appeared in the form of an old man resting alongside the road.

"Sir, do you know this road?" the pilgrim asked.

"That I do," said the angel.

"Then you've *seen* the city on the hill?" the pilgrim asked breathlessly.

"I've seen it," spoke the angel, "and He who dwells in it and lights it day and night by His presence."

Excited yet still worn out from his journey, the pilgrim said, "But sir, I've noticed the road climbs steadily uphill. Is it uphill all the way?"

"Yes, to the very end."

"And will the journey take all my days?"

"From morn till night, my friend."

For just a moment, the pilgrim's countenance fell as he thought of the struggle ahead. But then his eyes were brightened by the hope within him and the goal before him. He lifted his eyes to the uphill climb ahead and said, "Then I'll be back to my journey. *I shall be more and more tired, but also nearer and nearer to the One I most want to see.*"

That's actually a 100-year-old sermon illustration used by a pastor who has long since reached the end of his journey. Like him, we may end up weary and worn from the uphill struggle of creating and practicing our plan of action, but we'll be closer and closer to that city on the hill each day.

How about you? Are you ready to keep going in a long, uphill journey? Our prayer as you seek to make godly changes is that you'll move closer to your Savior and loved ones, and that on the last day of your life, your family and friends will say of you, "He was a man who stayed the course and went the distance for God."

See You at the Finish Line

by
Pete Richardson

My grandpa leaned over his hospital bed and grabbed my hand. His 6'2", once-solid frame was now withered to feather weight after battling brain cancer. God had softened his heart over the previous three months, and my dad, a strong Christian since he was 16, had the privilege of leading Grandpa to Jesus on the last lap of his life—after years of rejecting the Good News.

Now just days from death, he muttered his last words to me: "Pete, I only have one regret. If I had a chance to live life all over again, I'd have listened to your dad a long time ago."

I was only in tenth grade at the time and wasn't sure how to reply. I muttered, "It's okay, Grandpa. This is just the beginning."

Granted, Grandpa didn't walk with Jesus all his life. He was the epitome of a self-made man (he even looked like the Marlboro Man). But his heart melted before God on his deathbed. Grandpa may have been on the wrong track most of his life, but he crossed the right finish line! I'll always remember him as a man who finally yielded to God.

How Will You Be Remembered?

Have you ever read the epitaphs on tombstones? I don't make a habit of it, nor do I mean to be morbid. But my wife, Janet, and I used to live in Massachusetts, and occasionally we would read the epitaphs in the cemeteries from the 1600s to 1800s. Old-time New Englanders believed the logical place to have their final say was on their gravestones. Their often-stunning frankness gives the reader a glimpse into the character and mission of the deceased (for good or for bad). Here's an example from the book *Over Their Dead Bodies*:

HERE LYS YE BODY OF MR
DANIEL NOYES WHO DIED MARCH
YE 15TH 1716 AGED 42 YRS
4 MOS & 16 D-YS.

AS YOU WERE, SO WAS I
GOD DID CALL AND I DID DY
NOW CHILDREN ALL WHOSE NAME IS NOYES
MAKE JESUS CHRIST
YOUR ONLY CHOYES.

In his book *Straight Talk*, Dr. James Dobson tells of a conversation he had with his dad shortly before his death: "At one point, I turned to my dad and asked spontaneously, 'What do you want for an epitaph at the close of your life?' He thought briefly and then replied, 'Only two words: "He prayed"'" (p. 232).

How would you like your life to be summarized? If you could write your epitaph, how would it read?

Desire to Win

If you want to finish well, you must train well.

I'll never forget when I learned this vital lesson. I was a 14-year-old, 6'1" freshman playing in my first "C" squad basketball game. I don't remember all the details, but I do remember the cold sweat I felt sitting on the bench when the coach called, "Richardson! You're in."

I checked into the game, my mind reeling, trying to recall what defense we were playing and what position I was taking. Then it happened. I caught the ball, dribbled out in front of the pack, and tripped over my own size-12 feet at center court, crashing to the floor.

After the game, as I was leaving the gym, a classmate approached and said, "What'd I tell you—you'll never be a basketball player. What a waste of height!"

Whew! Those were powerful words for an already self-conscious teenager—enough to tempt me to cash it in and walk away from basketball.

The turning point came that evening, however, in a conversation with my dad. He knew I'd had a tough game, but he also knew what I needed. He asked me, "How bad do you want it?"

"Want what?" I asked.

"The game of basketball."

"What do you mean?"

"You must want it. You must have desire—desire to go for it. Desire to practice. Desire to pay the price. I don't see that desire in you."

In the following months, my dad reinforced his point. "Where's your desire?" he would ask almost daily.

His challenge made me rise to the occasion. I built my own court, went to summer camps, and practiced for hours each day, implementing what I learned. I repeated drills endlessly, working on the basics, wanting to master them. One year after the tripping episode, I couldn't wait to tell my dad that I had made the varsity team!

If properly applied, the same desire to win that's vital in athletics can provide more than good experiences. It can also lay the foundation for the competition that really counts—the one Paul referred to in 1 Corinthians 9:24-27:

> Do you not know that in a race all the runners run, but only one gets the prize? Run in such a way as to get the prize. Everyone who competes in the games goes into strict training. They do it to get a crown that will not last; but we do it to get a crown that will last forever. Therefore I do not run like a man running aimlessly; I do not fight like a man beating the air. No, I beat my body and make it my slave so that after I have preached to others, I myself will not be disqualified for the prize.

Paul's use of such athletic metaphors was undoubtedly rooted in the Greek tradition of his day, but the application was his. The primary point was Paul's challenge in verse 24, "Run in such a way as to get the prize." He was urging the Corinthians to "run" the Christian life in such a way as to obtain an eternal reward. The Corinthians showed their lack of "self-control" by insisting on their right to participate in idolatrous eating rituals in pagan temples. Paul exhorted them to refrain from such activity and warned them about the consequences—the real possibility of arousing the Lord's anger (see 1 Cor. 10:22; Gordon Fee, *The First Epistle to the Corinthians*, pp. 434-35).

Paul wasn't saying that only one receives the prize, as though the Christian life were a competition of some sort. Nor did he mean we must earn our salvation. Rather, he was saying, "Run the race as though you desire to win!"

Which race are you running, God's or another? Is your desire in the Lord? Are you running as if you want to win?

Focus on the Prize

Any athlete who participated in the Greek Olympic games was required to go through 10 months of strict training and was subject to disqualification if he failed to do so (Fee, p. 436). Paul applied this training to the Corinthians and to himself. In their situation, it meant not simply forgoing some rights for the sake of others (as in 8:7-13), but also forgoing some things altogether because they're inherently incompatible with the Christian "race" (see 10:14-22).

To press his point, Paul contrasted the forms of the prize. The athlete goes through such discipline to receive the victor's "crown," a "perishable wreath." In contrast, Christians get a crown that will last forever—the eternal victory of salvation itself. It is of such value that it should affect the way we live.

Paul applied this principle to himself in the negative: "Therefore I do not run like a man running aimlessly; I do not fight like a man beating the air" (1 Cor. 9:26). In other words, he had a fixed goal and was intensely focused on the prize. He exercised self-control as part of that focus, lest he be "disqualified for the prize" (v. 27). To run with no eye on the prize is as useless as getting into the ring only to box air. For Paul, everything was for the sake of the gospel, that he, too, might share in its blessings.

What will you receive when your life is over? Will it be the prize God has prepared for you in Christ or something else? Are you willing to train well so you might finish well?

Stay the Course

Throughout this book, the writers have challenged us to move beyond promise making to promise keeping. As Coach McCartney said, we must approach God in brokenness and humility. We must be aware of the potential barriers, as Dr. Gary Oliver explained, and we must understand the process Dr. John Trent has articulated so well. As each author of the chapters on the seven promises revealed, Christian maturity (Christlikeness) is the result of passing the tests, the trials and temptations of life, by leaning into Jesus when we stumble. Christian growth is a process. We must give ourselves space and grace. But we must also run the race with a desire to win, focused on the prize.

At Promise Keepers, we recognize there's a danger that men will interpret the seven promises as a list of commandments that can't be kept. So let me be clear that that's not our intention. The seven promises summarize our values as a ministry and raise the standard for what it means to be a godly man. They're meant to guide us toward the life of Christ so that He, in a life-long process, might transform us from the inside out.

This kind of transformation is the most important vital sign for Promise Keepers. It's also the most difficult to measure. How do you monitor the extent of God's work in a man's heart, which in turn affects his family, church, community, and ultimately his nation?

As we grow through this process, we need the grace and strength of the Holy Spirit. Only then will we become more like Jesus Christ and exert a godly influence in our relationships and world. The ultimate goal of our ministry, then, is to help men become living, practicing promise keepers.

We recognize that before a man becomes a "promise keeper," he must be a "promise seeker." The seeking process leads a man to God Himself and His promises. At that point, a man must become a "promise receiver." Embracing and owning the promises of God provides a foundation for a man to become a "promise maker." Finally, by God's grace and power, he lives the rest of his life as a "promise keeper."

In other words, promise keeping is a process, and it's vitally connected to a man's relationship with Jesus Christ.

Promise Seeker → *Promise Receiver* → *Promise Maker* → *Promise Keeper*

By now, you've identified where you are in relationship to the seven promises, and you've listed key action points and potential barriers. This planning process is as important as the final plan itself. And a Christ-centered plan—if executed—is a blueprint for godly change.

Now determine to stay the course. Be quick to get back on track when you find yourself veering off. Desire to win. Focus on the prize. Stay the course.

Guard Your Heart

If unity breeds strength, divisiveness breeds weakness. Abraham Lincoln understood this. He knew it wasn't the chance of an enemy invasion from overseas that threatened the integrity of the Union. Rather, it was division within. In his "A House Divided" speech, which he delivered on June 16, 1858, in accepting the nomination as a candidate for U.S. senator, he said:

> A house divided against itself cannot stand. I believe this govern-
> ment cannot endure, permanently half slave and half free. I do
> not expect the Union to be dissolved—I do not expect the house
> to fall—but I do expect it will cease to be divided.

It's no different in the Body of Christ. A divided church is a weak church; a unified church is a highly effective church. It's also the same with our heart—a heart divided is vulnerable and weak. Jesus said, "No one can serve two masters. Either he will hate the one and love the other, or he will be devoted to the one and despise the other" (Matt. 6:24). Solomon understood this principle when he wrote Proverbs 4:23: "Above all else, guard your heart, for it is the wellspring of life." These are serious words from a dad who was near the end of his life, leaving his son a summary of his wisdom. He was saying, "Listen up. What I'm going to say is the most important thing I'll ever tell you."

And what did Solomon say? "Guard your heart." Used as a metaphor in the Hebrew, *heart* refers to the inner nature of a man—the center of one's spiritual and intellectual life. Jesus said, "The good man brings good things out of the good stored up in his heart, and the evil man brings evil things out of the evil stored up in his heart. For out of the overflow of his heart his mouth speaks" (Luke 6:45).

What does it mean to "guard our hearts"? The question presumes our hearts need protection from some sort of enemy. Peter warned, "Be self-controlled and alert. Your enemy the devil prowls around like a roaring lion looking for someone to devour. Resist him, standing firm in the faith" (1 Pet.

5:8-9). Satan's mission is to disqualify us from the race, to take us out. So beware! As military sentries guard their posts, guard your heart.

Guard it with God's Word. Guard it by focusing on the prize set before you. Guard it by leaning into the grace of God, embracing your identity as His son. Guard it by keeping in step with God's Holy Spirit, being filled daily.

The opening scene in the movie *First Knight* is gripping. In a carnival-like setting, Lancelot badgers the onlookers to produce any sword-fighter who can withstand his skills. After a silent moment, a tall, blond young man named Mark steps forward and draws his sword. Their blades clash. It's obvious this guy can fight. But just when you think Lancelot has found his match, he makes his move and flips the sword out of Mark's hand. As the crowd cheers, Mark approaches Lancelot and asks, "How do you do that?"

Lancelot replies, "Three things. Number one: You've got to know your enemy. Number two: You've got to anticipate his next move. And number three: You can't care whether you live or die."

Know your enemy! Know his moves! Realize that the devil will seek to disqualify you by enticing you with "the cravings of the sinful man, the lust of the eyes and the boasting of what he has and does" (1 John 2:16). Eugene Peterson in *The Message* paraphrases it this way:

> Don't love the world's ways. Don't love the world's goods. Love of the world squeezes out love for the Father. Practically everything that goes on in the world—wanting your own way, wanting everything for yourself, wanting to appear important—has nothing to do with the Father. It just isolates you from him. The world and all its wanting, wanting, wanting is on the way out— but whoever does what God wants is set for eternity. (1 John 2: 15-17)

Beware! The enemy will bait you to want your own way, to want everything for yourself, and to want to appear important. As one preacher said it, beware of falling prey to one or more of the "three g's": girls, gold, and glory.

Don't be caught celebrating yet, because the war is still on. The enemy wants to entice you any way he can. He wants to deceive you, plunder you, and disqualify you from the prize set before you. Guard all the gates into your heart—that part of your inner man that thinks, feels, and wills—for out of it comes the fullness of what it means to live a faithful, godly life.

See You at the Finish Line

What might happen if you focus on the prize and run the race with unswerving passion to win? What might happen if I make the same commitment? What might happen if thousands of other men join us? What about millions? What might happen if we all go the distance?

I'll tell you what: Let's start with you and me.

Focus on the prize.

Desire to win.

Stay the course.

Guard your heart.

Together, let's determine, by God's grace and strength, to go the distance and end well. With a clear conscience, I want to be able to instruct those who make my tombstone to have it read, like that of the Reverend Bunker Gay who died in 1815,

> BE THOU FAITHFUL UNTO DEATH
> AND I WILL GIVE THEE A CROWN OF GOLD.
> I HAVE FOUGHT A GOOD FIGHT,
> I HAVE FINISHED MY COURSE.

About the Contributors

Charles W. Colson is founder and president of Prison Fellowship in Reston, Virginia.

Jack Hayford is pastor of The Church on the Way in Van Nuys, California, and a member of the board of directors of Promise Keepers.

Bill McCartney is the founder of Promise Keepers.

Jesse Miranda is associate dean of the School of Theology at Azusa Pacific University, a professor in the department of ministry, and a board member of Promise Keepers.

Gary J. Oliver, Ph.D., is the clinical director of Southwest Counseling Associates in Littleton, Colorado, an associate professor at Denver Seminary, and a member of the board of directors of Promise Keepers.

Luis Palau is an international evangelist and president of the Luis Palau Evangelistic Association in Portland, Oregon.

John Perkins is the founder of the Christian Community Development Association and publisher of *The Reconciler* magazine.

Randy Phillips is the president of Promise Keepers.

Pete Richardson is the vice president of communication services for Promise Keepers.

Gary Smalley is the president of Today's Family in Branson, Missouri.

John Trent, Ph.D., is the president of Encouraging Words in Phoenix, Arizona.

Stu Weber is the pastor of Good Shepherd Community Church in Boring, Oregon.

Acknowledgments

This book would not have been possible without the dedicated work of many people. Promise Keepers would like to recognize and thank them publicly for their efforts.

Jim Gordon, Manager of Publications, Promise Keepers.

Mary Guenther, Acquisitions Editor, Promise Keepers.

David Halbrook, Manager of Editorial, Promise Keepers.

Rod Cooper, National Director of Educational Ministries, Promise Keepers.

Dan Schaffer, National Manager of Field Ministries Training, Promise Keepers.

Al Janssen, Director of Book Publishing, Focus on the Family.

Larry Weeden, Senior Editor, Focus on the Family.

Tonya Christman, Administrative Assistant in Publications, Promise Keepers.